ॐ

BLUEPRINTS

FOR

POSITIVE LIVING

ॐ

William R. Jach

BLUEPRINTS

FOR

POSITIVE LIVING

by
William R. Jackson,
Ph.D.

JACKSON RESEARCH CENTER
P.O. BOX 3577
EVERGREEN, COLORADO 80439

ISBN: 978-0-9635741-4-5

10 9 8 7 6 5 4 3 2 1

First Edition

COVER DESIGN AND "LETTER" DESIGN:
Richard Stahlberg, Stahlberg Photography,
Martinez, California

INTERIOR DESIGN:
Dianne Nelson, Shadow Canyon Graphics,
Golden, Colorado

PRINTED IN THE UNITED STATES OF AMERICA
BY WALSWORTH PUBLISHING COMPANY,
MARCELINE, MISSOURI

Introduction

༂

Blueprints for Positive Living was created as a combined project by Dr. William R. Jackson and his father, Richard W. Jackson, to provide an innovative, spiritual GPS for our lives. They believe that people are a triunity comprising the subconscious mind, the conscious mind, and the superconscious mind. The superconscious is our spiritual and intuitive mind, and it is our connection with the divine.

Philosophy as an art can be an important teacher but often presents complex concepts that are hard to grasp. The authors' vision in this book is to help those of us whose minds and hearts are open to wisdom but need to understand our day-to-day lives through simple, direct truisms.

In *Blueprints for Positive Living,* we learn lessons about numerous issues—including wisdom, love, anger, beauty, business, character, and happiness, to name only a few. Some might leave you pondering an idea, others feeling compassion and affection, and still others generating a good, hearty laugh.

We suggest that you read these adages either from start to finish or by choosing a word that fits your mood for a particular day. However you approach your reading, may you find a ray of joy and enlightenment to help guide your everyday life.

It is a unique adventure when a father and son wordsmith together and share with others their insights on positive living through the use of one-of-a-kind sayings. It is their hope that this book will bring hope, courage, wisdom, and perhaps some much-needed laughter into the lives of those who venture into the words written here.

❧
Ability

There is more potential in every man under the false-bottom trunk of self-doubt than even his best friends surmise. Don't sell the trunk for a song!

❧
Achievement

Dream your dreams of achievement, but dream that you are working when you awake.

The Good Fairy with the magic wand said she couldn't loan it out anymore; but she did leave a pair of work shoes, a sweatshirt, and a bag full of potential achievement with the word "work" written all over it.

Achievement is its own reward, and accomplishment adds luster to any setting sun!

Do more than can be readily forgotten, and do it so well that even the calloused critics give their begrudging praise.

❧
Acquaintance

Great men may be better known through their
writings than by their neighbors next door.
How many great people do you know?

Men and women are like abandoned gold mines.
Reopen the tunnels of friendship and dig deeper.
You will find the treasures of true
acquaintanceship long neglected but
worth their weight in gold.

❧
Acquiring

To retain a fortune inherited is to earn it.

❧
Acting

Most men can play the fool without special practice,
having played the part before.

❧
Action

Action may appear magnificent,
but it is measured by its motive.

In the grammar of success, verbs count more than
adjectives, and description must follow action,
not substitute for it.

Only action or an act of God can perform miracles.
If you're not sure of one, work on the other.

&

Admiration

We admire in others the reflected image of ourselves if it
be noble, and despise it if it is not.

&

Adversity

Money can make a man feel rich, and adversity can make
him feel poor, but only courage can make him face facts
and forge new circumstances.

One end of adversity has horns; the other end produces
the milk of experience and the cream of wisdom.

It is easier to sympathize with the adversity of
another than to bear uncomplainingly
those misfortunes of our own.

There is no adversity equal to the loss of faith,
hope, or love.

Adversity is often the personal prescription provided
by the Divine Diagnostician.

Trouble cracks a mean whip, and memory holds
the sting, but neither helps the dullard who refuses
to be profited by it.

A soft bed and a secure future dull
the minds of millions who are content
with mediocrity. Adversity is the hard bed
and the sharp thorn that make men rise to labor
and to better serve their fellow men.

Adversity looks like the end of the road,
but just around the bend the fruit of adversity
hangs ripe on every tree. Stay until you
can see around the corner!

Adversity teaches with a hard rod, but the wise
remember the lessons that lead to
progress and prosperity.

☙

Advice

Those who ask advice too often really seek approval.

To demonstrate effectively is better
than to advise too freely.

❧
Age

Life is for action, youth is for learning,
and age is for memories without regret.

He who has a prune for a face is better
than he who has one for a heart.

Age should add smoothness
to the wine of our experience
and zest to our love of life.

Our years should measure growth and
maturity, ripeness and resourcefulness,
and not just the passing of our days.

A man is only old when his
vital juices turn sour and he lives
only to complain with
monotonous repetition of the
injustices and tyrannies of life.

Let the calendar count your achievements,
not your seasons only.

Let the clock hands point to the high noon
of your ambition, but never let them toll the
death knell of indecisive hours.

☙

Ambition

Honor and ambition should be early wed
and never divorced!

Blind ambition carries a heavy load down the wrong
road, but, once enlightened, it chooses the
right road but not the light load.

There is no place in heaven for covetous ambition
and no vault in a casket for its ill-gotten gains.

Ambition's empty substance, like the fabric
of a dream, can cast no eternal shadow
where it falls, save God be in it.

Ambition to be seen simply for self-exhibition is
unworthy. Ambition to serve without recognition is
unnatural. But ambition to achieve, to serve, to improve,
and to arrive—seen or unseen—is true ambition.

Too many people are asleep under the shade
of the family tree. Individualism plus ambition
will get up, move over, get its feet planted,
and learn to cast its own shadow.

The rundown man, like a rundown watch,
needs to be wound up often, shaken gently,
and watched occasionally.

12

Do you want to be a man, a mouse, or just
a miserable mistake? Choose one. Or, if you prefer,
you can be a miserably mistaken, male mouse.

Self-making, love-making, home-making, friend-making,
and heaven-making are the makings of a truly
successful man and are aims worthy of pure ambition.
Money-making may be added, too, if it isn't counterfeit!

☙

Anger

Ill temper is the father of ungoverned anger and the
mother of many mistakes.

Ill temper is cancerous; anger is costly; but kindness is the
best social security and the antibiotic for hate.

An angry man is a tempest-tossed ship caught in the
storm of his own brewing.

Anger shouts of a man's confusion and frustration.
It spells out the degree of his weakness and
reveals the limits of his endurance.

He whose displeasure is uncontrolled is in
no position to control others.

Anger is emotional intemperance where
displeasure would suffice as well.

The angry man, drunk on the excess of ill emotion,
cannot walk with equilibrium the line of reason;
his unweighed words and tainted breath of hate
still further spell out his inebriation.

Those who hang out with anger in the evening
will have a hangover of hate in the morning.

Anger that keeps its mouth closed
keeps its teeth longer.

Don't let the breath of anger blow out
the light of reason; men have lost their way
in the dark and others their lives.

The man who opens his mouth in anger
has his mind half-closed in pride.

An angry man is an unthinking man who
can be controlled by the prudent.

Many opportunities for advancement have been
chucked into the disposal of unthinking anger.

Life energies are better spent in advancement
than in helpless anger.

The guilty, the greedy, and the angry all
displace discernment, self-control, and sound judgment
with the witless waste of excessive emotion.

Smoldering anger leaves only the ashes of ill health,
irritated minds, weakened wills, and
devitalized spiritual energies.

Nothing unfits a man for emergencies
like a fit of anger.

෯

Appearance

Appearance is the casket, not the corpse;
penetration peers inside and pays tribute
to the cadaver, not the encasement.

The man who has no self-respect for his
personal appearance lacks respect for the
good vision of his observers.

A first-rate man does not
permit his breath, his body, or his
clothing to appear secondhand.

The man who refuses to dress well
chooses to play the part of the
beggar, the clown, or the fool.

The man who takes a daily bath recognizes
the man who doesn't.

Many a man's outward appearance walks the
picket line of protest that reveals his inner condition;
no man should go on strike against himself.

⌘

Appetite

The poverty of our abstinence exceeds
the abundance of our sustenance.

⌘

Apprehension

Apprehension is misdirected attention.

A little apprehension is better
than calloused confidence.

⌘

Argument

If you are under water or in an argument,
hold your breath as long as you can;
in either case, it may save your life.

It is difficult to listen well with one's mouth
open too far in wonderment, too often
in interruption, or too wide in protest.

More illumination of reason and less emotional
dogmatism would reveal our agreements and
heal our major differences.

He who listens well learns much; and it is better
to ask intelligent questions than to give
unwanted answers.

Your reaction to misinformation, argument,
and anger is the true indication of
your judgment and your size.

An argument a day keeps success away!

Avoid arguments and feed your facts to the
foe intravenously.

The man with an open mind usually keeps a closed
mouth; and the man who argues last, lasts longest.

❧

Associates

The man who cooks carrion calls
the vultures to his feast.

Those who run with the champions lose their limp or
their lives; but the run is worth the risk.

Your associates are the billboards of your worth
and the ambassadors of your own self-evaluation.

It is most difficult to sleep with the dogs and
not the fleas, to eat in the henhouse and
avoid the lice, to herd sheep and avoid the ticks.
It is better to avoid some circumstances
than to carry a load of flea powder, lice
eliminator, and tick remover.

Those who practice with the bullfrogs
have been known to croak on occasion;
but good singers choose great teachers.

ॐ

Autumn

Laughing autumn leaps astride the shocks
of standing corn and paints each pumpkin
with the vine from which the leaves are shorn.
Then laughing autumn calls the sleet
and frost while north winds coldly blow
and cover up autumn's painted pride
with impartial winter's mantled snow!

Babbler

Don't spend your tongue as though it were endless,
lest some should think it is!

Bag

The emptier the bag, the louder the rattle.

Beauty

Beauty is a sun, a smile, the light.
But both must quickly fade in error's night.

O, woman, why should beauty on
deception's brow be worn?

A happy heart is the finest facial.

Goodness and truth have beauty all their own;
but beauty hath not always good and truth alone.

❧

Bee

A bee will find some honey in a
poisonous flower; so men may wrest
some good from evil's power.

The gossip like the bee hath a
stinger in its tale; but no honeyed words
can change its ill intent.

❧

Begging

The beggar finds more pleasure here on earth
than those who have left it.

❧

Belief

The man who looks for light will find
the lamp; and he who for belief aspires
will find the facts for faith.

❧

Bells

The bells of memory, ringing clear, oft hurt
the heart but not the ear.

❧

Books

In the immortality of books the dead speak
yet once again and twice as loud and clear.

Books are the pure distillation of the mind,
undiluted by the frailty of the flesh that held the cup
where inspiration's dews first fell.

In the brotherhood of books, no bigotry
can close the door, for wisdom reaches out
its hands to every creed or race both rich and poor.

No man who writes a book can fully die,
for he has written with his blood
a message on the sky.

Books speak with thunderous tones from age to age;
man has no power to match the printed page!

❧

Business

Better to mind or mend your own business well
than to meddle with another's.

In business, all things are bought and sold
and with them the souls of men.

Business is more than busyness;
it is the commerce of service.

You are not in business unless you are actively
engaged in "delivering the goods!"

The three peas in any business "pod-nership" are:
production, progress, and profit. Are you in business?

The man who is in business for others is
most truly in business for himself.

If you fall flat on your business face,
turn over quickly; it is easier to look up that way,
but don't lie there too long.

Morale, not merchandise, is the heart of business success.

A business must have a name and an address, but it
shouldn't run all day under the shade of the same tree.

Don't be hypnotized into inactivity by a stroke of good or
bad business. Start your motor again, read your road
map, and drive on to your ultimate destination.

There is no camouflage for want of customers;
and an empty store means an empty till.

"Duffers" come and go, but good workers come to stay.

William R. Jackson

Courage is the key, opportunity is the door,
and good business is the reward that frugality
and labor bestow on the enterprising man.

A consistently successful businessman
must have an extrasensory periscope that
can look with discerning eye over, under,
or around all obstacles that may impede
his progress.

A business, like a wheelbarrow, is usually
at a standstill until somebody with ambition
pushes it along.

A good businessman should have one eye for present
opportunities and the other for future possibilities.

An indolent or discourteous clerk has already snapped a
padlock on the front door.

Stock your shelves with kindness, display each
product with courtesy, put a smile behind
every price tag, and the public will change
from window shoppers to cooperative customers.

A genial atmosphere, honesty in merchandising,
sincerity in service, and customer courtesy
keep the cash register ringing.

The Golden Rule is the distilled
ethics of good business; the more people
you help, the more people will help you.

Don't gang up on the customers,
or eventually the customers will gang up
on you; odds are they'll win!

Hire the man who can collect accounts and keep
the customers.

Customer interest neglected is customer interest lost.

Show the customer what you can do for him, and he'll
show you what he can do for you.

✍ Calumny

The best cure for scandal is to let it die,
unanswered and undisturbed.

Calumny is a hydra-headed monster; the louder you deny
it, the more vociferous heads arise to cry that scandal
denied must surely be true.

Calumny's malicious slander leaves a devastating trail of
destroyed reputation and blasted influence wherever its
hoarse whispers of hate and the scorched breath of its
falsehood by chance or intent are blown!

✍ Capacity

The gourmet, the camel, and the balloon have great
capacity, but quality is more important than quantity; for
a man must be full of more than food, water, or hot air.

The man who would trade a long life for a full stomach
gives evidence of an empty head.

❧
Care

The dog who chews a rubber bone all night
is too tired to eat in the morning!

No path is wide enough for true courage and
cowardly care to walk long together.

Worry goes to bed with its work shoes on,
still heavy with the toils of the day.

❧
Carelessness

Carelessness is as costly as crime, and some
have hung for it.

The careless sit on a powder keg with a short,
sputtering fuse.

❧
Causes

Trivial causes may produce terrific effects, for little is
much if trouble is in it.

The cause is always king and circumstance the servant;
and he who would change a decree must consult
with the Crown.

ॐ
Caution

Courage, like steel, is tempered with caution, but too much can ruin the sharpest blade.

If buyers were deaf or salesmen were mute, we'd look once, think twice, and ask for "something to-boot."

ॐ
Censure

It is better to be constructively censured than to be deceptively praised.

Censure, calmly and kindly given, provokes little contention, for its gentle persuasion speaks more clearly of its just judgment by the absence of its excessive emotion.

ॐ
Chance

Chance is the horse that those who are confident ride if it's going in the right direction when it passes by.

Chance, horseshoe luck, good fortune, and a benevolent providence account for more of our successes than our unfortunate pride will admit.

❧

Change

If life demands change, let judgment dictate its direction
and integrity its quality.

Adaptability, not capriciousness, is a virtue
in a changing world.

❧

Character

The weak will—undisciplined, unlearned, or ill taught—is
no proper foundation for character.

Character is the chain of sand, or the wrought-iron design
that action, interaction, providence, personal choice,
morality, and adversity have forged in the
fires of fear and faith.

❧

Charity

Charity responds eagerly to necessity while caution holds
court with the mathematicians.

Only what is given gladly on earth is retained as treasures
in heaven.

Charity is the beneficence of love in action; it is patience without petulance, kindness without calumny, self-respect without pride, progress without impropriety, ambition without selfishness, tolerance without termination, thought without iniquity, emotion without misdirection, burden bearing without blaming, faith without limits, hope all encompassing, endurance uncomplaining; and it is the greatest jewel in the crown of completeness!

ॐ

Cheerfulness

A smile runs on jubilant feet while sadness drags its crutches and complains.

Without the oil of gladness, the machinery of the mind and body complains and grinds incessantly and is the sooner worn away.

Cheerfulness is the sun in sorrow's night, with faith and hope its constant light.

ॐ

Ciphers

A cipher has rotundity, continuity, a periphery, and nothing to encompass. There are many citizens in Cipherville!

❧
Cities

What is a city but people; not tall skyscrapers with bright lights at night, but an ocean of surging, searching people—this is a city.

❧
Civility

The courtesy and consideration of polite civility often require no cost but quietness in the language of unspoken goodwill.

The chill of severe civility may be only courteous impoliteness; and what is overdone may be best left undone.

❧
Civilization

Degenerate civilization is little more than informed savagery; and without true piety, civilization is simply heathenism spelled in neon signs!

❧
Cleanliness

He who wallows with the pigs is unwanted in the parlor.

Cleanliness has its own rewards; but the dirty punish
both themselves and others.

Cleanliness begins in the order and purity of a righteous
heart, but it must not stop there.

A clean body encourages and invigorates a clean mind;
for cleanliness and character are compatible.

The window display represents the quality of the
merchandise inside the store as cleanliness of body
and propriety of dress advertise the hidden wares
of mind and spirit.

It is hard to smell the roses with a skunk loose
in the garden.

The man who munches garlic should brush his breath as
well as his teeth.

The confessional is the laundromat for washing souls.

౼

Clergyman

A politician behind a pulpit doesn't make a minister.

A preacher should be as upright and as rugged as the
cross he represents.

A minister should lean on his backbone and not on the pulpit, for he who has a cause will have a crowd.

Many a ministerial cupboard, like Old Mother Hubbard's, is too often bare except for an occasional bone of contention.

A minister's life is about as private as a person growing marijuana in a glass house across from the police station.

Some preachers push people toward perfection; others climb the heights and lift their followers after them.

The clergy as a profession attracts the wise and the otherwise, the good and sometimes good-for-nothing, some counterfeits, charlatans, and "saints in cellophane"; but, thank God, some ministers are the genuine, sincere servants of God and the people every day of the week and twice on Sunday!

The minister who loves leisure is saving himself, not souls.

༺

Cleverness

Adroitness is paid by the hour, cleverness by the week, ingenuity by the month; but persistent labor has an annual wage.

William R. Jackson

Cleverness is quick-witted contrivance, but labor lasts
longer; combined, they endure forever.

❧

Clock

The clock hands only point the hours and hide the face in
shame, devoid of other active powers for works
of praise or blame.

The clock has more ticks than a sheep, fewer numbers
than a lottery, a face without features, and one hand
is shorter than the other; yet it counts accurately
something more valuable than gold, tells silently
what everyone wants to know, is never two-faced,
serves as the chief regulator of society,
and is civilization's most alarming dictator!

The clock can measure time,
but only ambition can fill it.

❧

Clothes

A well-dressed man is known by the company of the
tailor he keeps.

A new suit with shoes unshined defeats the purpose one
has in mind.

33

Self-confidence, poise, and the proud carriage
of courage make an old suit look like a new one
and the man in it ten years younger.

A new trousseau and clothes fresh from the
cleaners are difficult to tell apart except
for the inner satisfaction of economy.

૭

Comfort

Comfort is the cure for grief, the soothing
balm of pain, redress for wrong, and surcease
for sorrow when love softly falls as the rain.

The person whose body is relaxed, whose mind is
contented, whose spirit is bathed in peace and dried
on the towel of courage, can put on the housecoat of
perfect love, the slippers of restful relief, and sip
the cup of comfort in quiet enjoyment.

૭

Commerce

True commerce is the flow of merchandise
from industry to industry, from individual
to individual. It is the interchange of ideas,
of action, of brain, brawn, and labor,
of goods, service, and silver.

Commerce is the building, binding, buying,
selling, bartering business of bestowing benefits for
a profit and by necessity to meet the multitudinous
needs of the beehive humanity.

❦

Common Sense

Common sense is that intuitive perception that sometimes
writes its reasons in shorthand but spells out its conclusions
in capital letters of judicious decisions.

Common sense can survive education and be profited by
it; but education cannot produce it or survive without it.

❦

Communism

Communism elevates mediocrity, fears individuality,
abolishes property, breeds inefficiency, exploits
excellence, undermines morality, mocks spirituality, mass
produces inequity, trades inequality for human dignity. It
is the rattle of chains for the bells of freedom and
uninformed bondage for life and liberty.

❦

Companions

Disease is contagious, but health is not; and it is easier to
avoid bad company than it is to cure bad habits.

❧
Compensation

Unjust causes produce unwanted circumstances, for compensation is the law of life.

As the child resembles the father, so our present and our future bear the birthmarks of our yesterdays.

Most consequences are but the late harvest of our early plantings, whether bad or good.

❧
Complaining

The complainer is a victim of his own "stomach complaint;" in other words, he's a "bellyacher" belching up his own bitter brew.

The complainer, like a neglected child, has a sour smell; what he really needs is a change of environment.

The complainer moans about the hangover his own intemperance caused, forgetting that it is his own painfully sensitive condition that makes common disturbances seem unbearable.

❧

Compliment

Neither the fawning compliments of underlings nor the congratulations of assumptive superiority are as acceptable as the sincere admiration of our relative equals.

❧

Compromise

Concession too cheaply given may be
too costly to keep.

Too costly is the compromise that gives
its foundations away.

Compromise is the barter of concessions among contending equals; but the one who gives an inch in compromise may gain a mile in purpose.

❧

Concealment

To conceal is to reveal; for the desire for concealment often reveals the nature of the desires, and the nature of our desires reveals the desires of our nature.

❧
Conceit

Circumstances have a way of puncturing the
exaggerated balloons of our vanity, for conceit
deceives others far less than ourselves.

Life tends to reduce conceit to caution.

❧
Confidence

Confidence should be earned rather than too freely given.

The man who distrusts himself has difficulty in depending
on the veracity of others.

Self-confidence is the grandchild of ambition, the child of
achievement, and the father of success.

❧
Conquest

Self-conquest is safer than conquest, for it has fewer
subjects to conquer or control, and, in case of mutiny,
there is more likelihood of compromise than decapitation!

❧

Conservatism

A man is no conservative who wants simply to exchange
one bag of ideas for another equally bad bag just for the
sake of exchange.

As the moon changes and the sun rises, so men progress
and methods alter, but the conservative man works with
the laws of life rather than trying to put the moon where
the sun is, or to reverse the rotation of the earth on its axis.

❧

Contentment

Satisfaction counts its treasures with glad hands and
shares willingly with others what it gratefully possesses,
and it sings of its fullness until the heavens drop down the
dew of continued contentment.

❧

Conversation

It is far better to speak sparingly, but with interest, on a
topic of another's choosing, than to hold forth fluently in
one of your own.

Courteous silence is a compliment to the man who speaks, and rapt attention makes that compliment profound.

Hollow conversation shouts abroad that empty heads are holding idle hands while witless judgment fails to find the emergency brake for loquacious talk.

కా

Cooperation

Cooperation is a song where each must harmonize with the one who carries the melody. It helps to sing in the same key, on pitch, and in perfect time.

Cooperation is a scaffold for ability and for stability. Non-cooperation is simply a scaffold!

కా

Countenance

The face, like the preface of a book, may tell too little, too much, or nothing at all.

Like the table of contents in a history book, some faces reveal at a glance the abbreviated narrative of a life of good or ill, of fullness or vacuity.

Engraved on every countenance are the sculptured scars or the beauty lines of each hidden thought or deed.

ॐ

Courtship

Never court so vigorously as to alarm,
nor so vaguely as to be misunderstood,
nor so as to pass the buying signals
of acquiescence when they come.

He who courts endlessly without conquest
fails to court well; and he who ceases to court
after conquest is a poor winner and a bad debtor.

ॐ

Covetousness

Greed makes want's vacuum greater but can
never fill it up.

No covetous gain is great enough to cure the affliction of
greed, for it is the sickness of selfishness and the dementia
of distraught desires.

ॐ

Cowardice

If you think with your legs, you may find them
too idle to run, too weak to escape, and too
cowardly to return; but one who thinks with
his heart thinks courageously!

꙳

Credit

The man with some cash has more credit.

A man without credit is a man who lost his life preserver before he learned how to swim.

Credit is character, confidence, integrity, industriousness, and dependability plus a banker who believes you have it.

Ninety-five percent of all business is conducted on credit. The man is really unfortunate who hasn't saved the other 5 percent to start with.

Court your wife if you like, but court your creditors whether you like it or not, for he who doesn't pay court to his creditors will likely pay his creditors in court.

Carelessness costs credit, loss of credit costs opportunity, and a careless man without credit or opportunity is soon doing business on a vacant lot.

꙳

Creeds

The simplest creed is the creed of kindness, the tolerance of love, and the unity of understanding.

Creeds too often breed criticism, division, pride, separation, seclusion, and false superiority.

Creeds have value as the authoritative formulation of religious beliefs and doctrines and will agree or differ in accordance with purpose, understanding, interpretation of facts, principles, and personal opinions.

All creeds are cadavers without Christ for their lives, the Holy Spirit for their light, and the Bible for their foundation.

∼

Criticism

The heady wine of criticism loosens the tongue, closes the mind, and freezes the heart; so don't drink the conceit of criticism.

Too many people are already "knock-aholics."

Criticism costs confidence; even the critic's best friends find their own confidence ill at ease.

To encourage the good is better than to criticize the bad.

The carping critic is usually a competitor even as the ranting raver is a rival.

Criticism is a cancer, and the vicious are its victims; and
the criticized often outlive the critics.

Criticism cries aloud of its want of charity.

Self-improvement is easier than the reformation
of all humanity.

The critic who is secretly conscious of his own faults may
feel the necessity of proving the rest of the world wrong.

The false pride of the critic weighs its finger
on the scales of justice.

The swivel-tongued, carping critic has much to swear at
and so little to swear by.

~
Dad

A son confirms his mother's good judgment when
he loves and respects his father.

No son really knows how to appreciate his father
until he has been one, and then it is often too late.

~
Death

Death clings impulsively to the cold breast of receding
earth and only asks for life, not lust or mirth.

He fears no terror who in death resigns himself
to eternal life.

What is death but dust resplendent in resurrection's hour;
and what is death but the gate to heaven and the scepter
of deathless power?

To live nobly is to die well.

Why should the mortal dust not settle in
the shade whence once it arose; and why
should not clay return to the bank
where the river of eternal life flows?

There is no darkness to the saints in death;
only another dimension of light.

If a man owned the whole earth, it would not
be for long; after which he could occupy
only a few feet of it until time and
deterioration made the dust of the grave
and the dust of its owner without
distinction or identity.

~

Debt

Too many small debts make a man feel small; but a larger
debt wouldn't make him feel any bigger.

To sacrifice today and prosper tomorrow is better than to
live in comfort today on mortgaged tomorrows.

The best balanced mind has a balance in the bank.

The chronic beggar and the chronic borrower are blood
brothers, and they'll both bleed for it.

~

Decision

Decide wisely, begin promptly, and continue persistently, for such action spells out success.

The proper exercise of a virile, decisive, creative will is the mark of your own God-imaged divinity in the dimensions of humanity.

Delayed decision is the dawdler's dilemma.

We let others make our decisions for us so that we can escape the responsibility and still criticize them for their stupidity just in case.

Decisions are personal, and each man has the awesome right to determine his own destiny, his failure, or his success.

You are as good as you think you are, whenever you think you are; so try making your own decisions. Remember, after all, you are the president of You, Inc.!

Proposals, postponement, and procrastination are the treason triplets.

If good intentions were dollars, the whole world would be wealthy; but again, maybe that's why it isn't. Be decisive!

ॐ
Dependability

A man can get along without a formal education,
but he must know how to spell at least one word
correctly. That word is dependability, and he
must spell it out in actions every day.

ॐ
Destiny

Every man is breaking the sound barrier
to his future at the rate of sixty seconds a minute and
sixty minutes per hour. Do you know your destination?

Who knows what destiny is God's design, or what duties
were eternally ours to perform? To know this is our first
duty, and to do it is our life; nor will God neglect to guide
us in our knowing and in our doing.

ॐ
Determination

Determination, like the bulldog, never lets go except to
get a better grip on a more vital part.

Balkiness describes the mule; tenacity,
the bulldog; but wisely directed determination
is the trait of champions.

The flea tries to make up in activity what it lacks
in persistence.

A persistent man with poor tools will accomplish more
than a dullard with sharp ones. Application and
determination make the difference.

Determination fortifies courage, increases confidence,
energizes purpose, clears the vision, and strengthens
the will to win.

A man steps up or stumbles over his own attitudes on
the stairway to success. He must keep a determined and
positive outlook, and uplook, to arrive at the top.

Determination is a steadfast will in purposeful action.

Development

To achieve with humility is better than to succeed
with pride.

All things must blossom or wither, grow or die, for the
law of increase is the law of life.

Men find it difficult to find their niche in life because the
small places are already taken. The man who would fill a
large place must grow into it.

~

Disappointment

Disappointment may be like a burr under the saddle
blanket or a spur in the horse's flank, but no
man should give up because disappointment
galls or goads him. Our disappointments should
only spur us on to greater conquest.

Don't let life's disappointments disappoint you.
The places where you fall will soon be road markers
on your way to ultimate achievement.

When success seems a delusion and hope
a mirage, when the day seems all darkness
and you can't remember where you
were going or why, just remember that
the sun will rise again tomorrow morning,
or at least by day after tomorrow!

Shall we multiply disappointment by disappointing
our friends also? No, true courage thinks first of
others, picks up the broken pieces of failure,
and molds a mosaic in success.

~

Discipline

Discipline is a firm hand on a bridled mind.

Discipline is a track to run on with switches all closed, destination decided, and with will sitting tall and determined on the engineer's seat.

Discipline is the antidote for the poison of insubordination, irresponsibility, and irregularity.

Self-respect produces self-discipline, and self-discipline, in turn, increases self-respect.

Right regard results in rigorous restraint relative to all relationships.

Self-discipline is self-control. It is a prerequisite for cooperation, leadership, and survival itself.

∂

Discouragement

Dark days reflect the condition of our inner sight as much as the condition of our outer circumstances.

Discouragement is empty-handed frustration and fear.

Discouragement is a soldier that used all his ammunition and forgot there was a bayonet on his gun.

Never encourage discouragement. Deny it, belie it, court-martial it, and try it, but don't ever buy it!

Discouragement is the distemper of despondency, the disease of despair. Cure it; don't countenance it.

Discouragement is the tough kid who kicks the crutch out from under crippled hope. It snatches the purse of purpose, paralyzes the power of performance, and strangles the struggler. Run from it; fight it; but never embrace discouragement.

The mood of discouragement is more vicious than the circumstances that triggered it. Take a second look and you'll find a way out. Take another look and you'll see how lucky you really are.

❧

Disposition

Don't offset a day of smiles by one last unthinking frown.

The wise can be guided and fools can be led, but God Himself finds it difficult to correct the conceited!

❧

Dreams

Dreams are fanciful, beautiful, nebulous things. Dreams are luminous, airy, dazzling things. They are woven from the fabric of hope, the cobwebs of desire, and the gossamer wings of ambition envisioned.

Dreams are the blueprints for reality, the scaffolding for our skyscrapers, and the foundation of future fortunes. Don't chuck your cherished dreams in the disposal of doubt.

We peddle our dreams like paupers and display them where the hawkers cry; but if new dreams could be bought in the marketplace, I wonder whose dreams we would buy?

Hang the portrait of your intended accomplishments in the castle of your dreams, and awake each morning to make that dream come true.

ॐ

Duty

The person who discharges the duties expected will not be discharged for his duties neglected.

Yesterday is a cadaver; tomorrow is an unborn child; today alone is alive with opportunity and reward. Duties well done are the happy secret of each successful today and the proud parents of more glad tomorrows.

❧

Earnestness

Earnestness is eloquence with ability,
education, and attention sitting
enthralled at its feet.

Earnestness is a flame where even genius
warms its hands.

❧

Education

Education is the ability to evaluate
rather than to simply accumulate
knowledge.

Wealth of knowledge pays high interest
and suffers loss from no inflation, save pride.

Education is costly, ignorance is cheap,
but he who pays the least will
pay the most.

Money spent for foolish pleasure is an exchange for regret; but money deposited in the vault of education is the best investment yet.

Education is the interminable process of self-discovery, the bringing to light of our hidden treasure, and the enlargement of our capacity to still discover more.

Education doesn't start in school, nor does it end there. It is a lifelong process of self-correcting vision, judgment, and discipline.

The man who stops studying when he stops going to school is losing more than his hair.

Wisdom is the prize that fools never gain and the price that the indolent never pay.

֎

Egotism

Egotism is spawned in the darkness of ignorance and seldom learns how ill it appears in the limelight it loves.

The egotist twirls the baton of conceit in his parade of ignorance while the band marches down another street.

The egotist is a fool marching with the scholars without cap or gown on graduation day, unaware that his self-inflated opinion and the robe of wisdom were not both cut from the cloth of truth.

ॐ
Emotion

Books or bullets are only emotions materialized
and brought to light.

He who commands his emotions controls his life.

Emotion, the atomic energy of mind and spirit, is a power
plant for good or ill. It is life's vital force directed or
misdirected, negative or positive, constructive or
destructive. Emotion is what you make it, how you
direct it, and where and why you project it.

Inventory your emotions: don't overstock the shelves
of your inner self with less than the best or
with unwanted excess.

ॐ
Employment

Man's happiest employment is found in the area of his
greatest abilities and his deepest interests.

Employment and a job are not always synonymous. The
one is a task and the other is active involvement in the
accomplishment of it. In either case, the employee's
position should be one of application.

Activity and achievement are prerequisites of any continued employment. You can't maintain a "position" without changing your position. So hold your job up, don't hold it down!

❦

Encouragement

You can maintain your own standing
better by patting someone on the back
rather than by kicking them in the back side;
for the kicker has only one leg to stand on
and that not for long.

The larva crawls before it flies, and man reaches freedom
or the gallows by only one step at a time.

A frown may cost you more than a mile
of smiles can repay.

No hill is as steep or a mile as long if a friend or
companion is taken along.

❦

Enemies

An active enemy activates our energies,
and opposition stimulates the thyroid and
keeps us wide awake.

Criticism is a thorn in the side of complacency;
thus, even our enemies are helpful.

A friend fronts for our faults, but an enemy
forces us to face the facts of our
failures frankly.

࿇

Energy

Energy is the true coin of the kingdom.
You can't buy and sell without it.
It is the basis of credit, the currency
of commerce, the bonds in the bank,
the difference between failure
and success. Spend your energy where
it counts the most and costs the least.

Ability and judgment plus energy equal
achievement. Work is the watchword
and energy is the word to watch.

Purpose is the gun barrel, will is the trigger, and action is
the bullet; but energy is the powder that drives it
to the mark.

Energy is everywhere; breathe it in and work it out.
Interest and energy are Siamese twins; where one goes,
the other follows.

William R. Jackson

Enthusiasm

Enthusiasm is the outreaching, positive,
creative force of God within us manifesting
itself in the lively spirit of
joyous progress and increase.

Enthusiasm is confidence radiating,
faith achieving, and love expanding
in the glow of eager, interested service.

Enthusiasm is confidence at the bat, endurance circling
the bases, and the player sliding home. Enthusiasm has
the highest batting average and the best score.
Be enthusiastic.

Anybody with a checkbook can buy your merchandise,
but only the man with the facts, faith, and fervor of
enthusiasm can sell it.

Enthusiasm tempered with persistence and judgment will
steadfastly burn its way to any desired goal.

Enthusiasm is contagious power. Its high-frequency
vibrations are in tune with the energy pulsations
of all creation.

People and circumstances respond to the heartbeat of
enthusiasm in action.

ॐ
Environment

Failure is a wilted, half-eaten apple with a half-dead worm, where effort, not environment, failed first.

Conditions are crutches, environment is clay, and the strong mold monuments from circumstances that would crush less courageous, creative men.

Man should influence environment and not be victimized by it; he should evaluate, invigorate, and renovate his environment by resolute purpose, determined will, and energized action.

ॐ
Envy

It takes some ambition to even be envious.

The soul's moth-eaten garments by envy destroyed, might have been better preserved with charity employed.

The covetous, ill will of envy eats away at a man's own vitals instead of picking fruit from the tree of his own achievement.

Envy is emotional indigestion that can't enjoy its own menu because its neighbor is eating steak.

Envy is a foul fighter. It forgets fair play, espouses
falsehood, and viciously attacks the cause
of its discontent.

Envy is illness, contentment is comfort, and harmony
is better than a bag full of gold.

Envy is a conveyor belt that seldom
brings us the objects of our spiteful,
selfish, or unhappy desires, but deposits
instead a load of dubious discontent
and a case of incapacity to enjoy
what we already possess.

Avoid envy, expand the awareness of
your own good fortune, and cultivate
gratitude in the cheerful
climate of thoughtful thankfulness.

❧

Epitaphs

Many a knave's epitaph has already
been fashioned by his contemporaries,
and all epitaphs are not eulogies.

It isn't what others will write on your head stone that
counts as much as having the golden rule
written on your heart stone.

⌘
Eternity

Oh, eternity, that ocean without shore,
as bottomless and as deep as hell
and high as heaven, where tide and time
and measure are no more!

⌘
Examples

Who makes a law has helped to make restraint;
who sets a good example has helped
to make a saint.

Sermons are sayings sometimes written in the sand;
but character and conduct are monuments
chiseled in the solid rock.

Christ is the greatest example
and the Bible our greatest guide.

Sincerity's silent oratory is more eloquent than dramatic
discourse. The still, small voice of example shouts above
the storm of words.

Good examples are patterns of excellence more easily
read than books, more practical than advice, are difficult
to argue with, and often inspire imitation.

❧
Excess

To covet power is to court excess, and to covet knowledge proves either pride or humility; but he whose quest is love and love alone finds no excess; for love is a flower by temperance grown.

❧
Excuses

We are prone to excuse in ourselves what we rigorously condemn in others.

An excuse is a tongue-tied tattletale that can't tolerate the test of truth.

The more we try to excuse ourselves, the louder we cry of our failures.

❧
Experiences

Adaptation is the fruit of experience. Man learns by doing and by undoing, and he who participates wisely profits the most.

Wisdom councils with experience, and the past helps prove our proposals.

The man who buys the experience of others is wiser than
the one who must try all things for himself.

Bitter experience is the record of ruin,
the memory of misery, and the
wisdom awakened by folly.

Experience is the "sheepskin" a man earns
by being the "goat."

Rewarding experience reinforces our reactions even as
profitable participation proves our prudence.

෯

Extravagance

The wasteful, unreasonable excess of extravagance
thinks immoderation is freedom while it
forges the chains of failure around its feet.

To spend money foolishly is financial folly,
but to waste time and misdirect energy
is to lose life without living it.

Face

The face is first to speak an invocation and
acquaintanceship, or to make one want
to stand for the benediction.

Who knows how close the face
resembles fortune, reveals its lack
or cause, and cries its wares
when we had hoped them silenced.

The face is the mirrored parchment of the
mortal soul, and those who can or
care to read will need
no other scroll!

Facts

A wise or eloquent man must relish facts, like the
farmhand relishes food, if he is to produce
vigorous thoughts and effective labor.

The strength and depth of our wisdom, and
the extent and the permanence of our
achievements, depend upon the assimilation
and contemplation of the facts we store
in the vaults of our subconscious,
creative mind.

A faculty for facts is more fortunate
than a facility for fanciful fiction, foolish fabrication,
or fruitless fantasy; for the framework
and fabric of failure are founded on
falsehood, but facts fortify infallibility
and further favorable fortuity.

≈

Failure

The man who faces failure is looking
in the wrong direction!

The foreclosures of past failure may be the
forerunners of future fulfillment.

Never talk failure, trouble, or want.
We fortify the images that we
envision most. Identify yourself with
income, increase, and expectancy.
Let failure lie with the fallen;
up, on your feet, and press on!

Don't puncture your balloon of hope
with the barbs of remembered failures.

Incompetence, indifference, indolence, and loss of interest
are the pallbearers at the funeral called "failure."

The cold feet of failure, the empty hands of want, and the
beggar's garments of indolence are not fitting for a king.
The royal wardrobe provides for kingly occasions.

No failure need be final. In its bitter fruit are
the seeds of sweetest success.

॰ॐ

Fairies

The fairies ride the sunbeams to the ground
and hide behind the sunbeam shadows;
that's why they can't be found!

॰ॐ

Fairness

Fairness is akin to kindness, and
kindness is akin to God.

The fair-minded are fortunate, for the law
of compensation follows their footsteps
and furthers their noble designs.

Fairness is founded on the golden rule of love.

The test of a law is fairness,
with justice the foundation stone.

Your circle of influence expands
as your reputation for fairness increases.

Fairness strengthens friendship, and the fairness of a
leader forecasts his following.

Faith rests at the feet of fairness
where equity once stood alone.

༄

Faith

Faith is an inner faculty that sees the invisible,
hears the inaudible, touches the intangible,
and claims their bounties for its own.

The faith that sees the invisible will be rewarded by
demonstrations of visible sight; the faith that first can
hear the inaudible will bring forth the audible sound; and
the faith that can touch the intangible will find the fabric
of reality in its outstretched hands.

Faith is a laser beam of vital, spiritual force directed to
the illumination and direction of the affairs of life.

William R. Jackson

As fish without water find the swimming
rough, so faith without works is something,
but not enough!

Faith is the pivot of progress, the center of all
achievement, and the source of all inspiration.

Faith is a sure foundation and the rest to labor given;
it is the repose of confidence and hope that counts
on God and heaven!

Faith is an attitude of acceptance, confidence, and trust in
the integrity and dependability of a beneficent God
and a friendly universe.

Faith is an impregnable fortress secure even though the
entire world lies embattled at its feet.

Faith is an ocean where even hardships ride like leaves
borne up on its mighty tide.

The fabric of faith is interwoven in
all the intricate designs of society: in government, in
labor, in business, in education, in religion,
in morality, and in life itself.

Even the skeptical must live
by the measure of faith.

॰৶

Falsehood

Untruth is a hooded serpent's head where the glass
jewel of deception rests to tempt the greedy in their
risk of poisoned life and limb.

The feigned breath of Falsehood taints
the purest air, for Miss-Statement
woos with Error although she
seems at times most fair.

The soul should fumigate for
falsehood like the health
officer fumigates for some
pestilential ill.

Falsehood left to multiply in corners dark
will soon have its foul offspring gaping
at each windowsill.

It is better to go bare-handed
through any battle than to go hooded
by false deceptions or to wear the
crown of error and untruth.

He who deals in lies protects his hapless head with the
frail fabric of a falsehood and fails to find the forged-steel
helmet of veracity and truth.

⌒

Fame

Fame is the fragrance arising from great things nobly
done; but notoriety is the evil stench of folly
rotting in the sun!

With immortal fame, or a charmed name,
the dead wear well their laurels;
but who, forsooth, was great in truth?
Here fact with history quarrels!

Transient fame, like candle flame, goes out
when tempests blow.

We march in tribute to the great with
sounds of drum and fife; but does our
oft-belated praise infuse their
dust with life?

Fame is an empty tomato can, raised high, where envy
builds its nest and broods, as doubt's fledglings
raise their hunger cry.

⌒

Fate

Faith rides the horse called "Fate"
wherever it wishes or wills.

Destiny is determined by choice,
envisioned by faith, and achieved
by creative, persistent action and intention.

Fate is the product of our inner choosing,
the result of our intense desires,
the reward of our true expectations,
and the manifestation of our
just compensations.

No fortune cookie selects our future;
no goddess of doom decides our fate.
We attract from without what we radiate from
within; only our own comes to us soon or late.

❧

Faults

Be a faultfinder, but only in your own backyard.
The neighbors seeing your progress will be inspired
to begin their own reformation.

The faults we see in others are the magnified
mirrors of our own.

Speak not too often or too loudly
of the faults you see in others
lest your listeners observe these
same failings reflected in your face.

Despised tendencies within ourselves
vividly tint the same traits in the actions
of others, which we readily recognize and
condemn while unaware of our own
colorblindness to the same faults within ourselves.

☙

Fear

Caution is akin to fear when it
stops drinking its hot
coffee and starts blowing
on its iced tea!

Overcaution is a jailer who imprisons
our good intentions, handcuffs our
actions, and forgets on purpose
where it hid the keys.

Fear is a foe or fear is a friend;
hold it in the light while you decide
if you should keep it or drown it
in a bucket of faith.

Fear is an apparition, but don't believe every ghost or
goblin story that you hear.

The fearful and the foolish hold Halloween
365 days of the year.

False fear germinates in ignorance and grows in the
darkness where it fetters our feet, attacks our ambition,
kills our courage, and drives us stumbling from the
pathway of purpose into the deeper shadows of doubt
and despair. Never cultivate or coddle false fear.
Fumigate!

Dump your doubts, deny defeat, face your fears,
campaign for courage, affirm your faith,
and the whole world will help you win.

Fear is a rampant emotion, a runaway horse on the road.
Avoid fear and keep your own horses tied unless you are
in the saddle or in the driver's seat.

The exchange of futile fear for achieving faith, and
overcaution for courage, is the first order of business
for every day.

Don't order your coffin until you need it; you may not!

&

Feasting

He tends to gluttony who finds more enjoyment in his
food than in his friends.

A great deal may be learned about a man by the manner,
the amount, and the place of his eating.

Just as good food and vitamins are important for bodybuilding, so inspirational thoughts are essential for clear minds and strong character.

When the banquet begins, let Pleasure sit on your left hand and Temperance on your right hand. It's harder to overeat with someone sitting on both hands.

❧

Flattery

Flattery is a sincere compliment minus the sincerity.

Flattery wouldn't be tolerated except for the inherent, hidden hunger for approbation and praise; but the flatterer makes cheap merchandise of a valuable commodity for lack of true insight and sincerity, and for selfish ends.

❧

Flowers

Blooming flowers always hold a fragrant, heaven-like beauty of their own that seems to make the Great Creator say, "I'm just beyond the wall they're growing through; why not stand by me a moment here and pray."

Let us smell the aroma of the flowers and praise the goodness of our friends; both are worthy, and both are too soon gone.

Forgetfulness

Forgetfulness points a self-accusing finger at our
lack of interest or intention.

The forgetter will be forgotten,
and the efficient will take his place.

Send me a bouquet of forget-me-nots;
I have a whole row of forget-you-nots
growing in my garden.

Fortitude

The wounds that hurt too deeply for salves to heal
respond to time, which cures all pains we feel.

Fortitude and hardihood can win in the three-legged race;
and it's always better to have your feet tied
than your faith!

Foundations

A solid foundation and the steel girders of integrity,
purpose, and high ambition make the difference
between air castles and skyscrapers.

A just cause is a good foundation.

No life can rise as high or remain as unshaken
as the one that has gone deep enough to find the
foundation stones of integrity, faith, and service.

The establishment of a man, an institution, or a fortune
rests on the fulcrum of its foundation and is raised
by it as well as upon it.

~

Friendship

No man has truly conquered an enemy
until he has made him a loyal friend.

Friendships, like forged steel,
are fashioned in the furnaces of adversity.

Your friends are your true assets; save them like you
would save money. We all have rainy days.

Chance, good fortune, and even adversity may bring you
friends, but they can also take them from you; therefore,
count your friends like a miser counts his coins and add
one every day.

Friendships, like pottery, can be broken,
but love will cement them again.

The fraternity of friendship is open to the happy smile
and the warm hand of helpfulness.

Matriculate in friendship
and major in the mathematics of compatibility.

Friendship chooses with wisdom
and criticizes with care.

Friendship is a spaceship that crosses isolation's
interplanetary space.

The frontiers of friendship still call for the pioneering
spirit and the courage of the conquistadors.

Goodwill gains good friends,
and the neighbor's dog knows if you really like him.

The man who slaps you enthusiastically
on the back in the morning and stabs you
in the back before night was a kindergarten
dropout in the school of friendship and is
still playing truant from the facts of life.

Friends lost are enemies gained,
and there is no enemy like a friend betrayed.

The wine of friendship sparkles in the eye, sings in the
voice, warms the hands, and quickens the heartbeat.

William R. Jackson

Even an unfurnished house seems warm and full
with friendship in it.

Friendship has a secret language
of heart and hand and eye.

Each friend is a link in the chain of life,
and the man who loses a link loses part of his life.

❧

Future

The future, great with the child of promise, knows no
birth pangs until its hour is come; therefore, let us wait
patiently while we enjoy life's present blessings
and not anticipate our future pains.

The future, like a chalice of unfolding, floral gold, opens
up its silent petals; and if perfumed sweet or bitter,
God still the flower holds.

Gardens

A garden is a lovely plot, wind-swayed in the summer
sun, with God as the neighbor who leans on my fence
while we talk when the day is done.

Genius

The genius of the inner mind needs the building
material of facts, the hammer and nails of
purpose, the square of truth, the saw and
rule of correction, the labor of meditation,
the blueprints of design and construction,
and a little time to accomplish its inspired ends.

Genius is the awakened faculty of the higher self
which draws on the brain bank of all humanity and
upon the wisdom and goodness of God.

Genius is the hand of faith that feels in the darkness
until it turns on the light of inspiration.

80

Genius is the cultivation of the instinct to find buried
treasure where other great men dug for the gold;
it is the discovery that wisdom lies hidden
just on the other side of the conscious mind.

Genius is the creative capacity of the awakened intellect
in cooperation with the creative mind of God.

Genius, which results from the activated exercise
and outpouring of the subliminal faculties of the creative,
subjective mind, is inspired by the emotional
intensity of necessity and emergency and
must be controlled by judgment and reason,
for it contains within its vast powers
the possibility of self-deception.

The genius thinks with the other side of his brain and
simply listens and records with his conscious intellect;
thus, his own mind as well as the minds of others are
stimulated by creative and original thought.

A genius may be recognized by his brilliance and often by
his rejection as much as by his acceptance.

આ

Gifts

It is the gift, the manner and meaning of the giving,
and above all, the giver in back of the giving,
that makes the gift a cherished thing.

A willing gift is doubly blessed;
but he who gives himself gives best!

God Himself has taught us the art of giving
by divine practice, precept, and inner promptings.

≈

Glory

Glory, that eminence of fame, condition,
pleasure, pride, and honor, is a precarious pinnacle
and a position in which it is difficult
to maintain a proper balance.

The splendor of achievement, the light of recognition,
and the glory of exaltation are bright halos for the
humble, but they ill fit the proud.

Earthly fame, like a slipping halo of glory,
blinds a man's eyes so that he sees only the distorted
image of himself without giving attention to the whole
picture of life; and it covers a man's ears
until he hears only the commendations
and gives no credence to criticism,
however true.

Fleeter than the flight of a bat on the wing
is the brief hour of honor for a pauper or a king.

ॐ
God

The God who could design the beauty
of the peacock's tail can provide food
for the other end.

He who would find God need not change his location,
only his point of view!

All of life and the disposal thereof lie ultimately
in the hands of God.

The study of the reality, the being, and
the nature of God is the paramount
duty of every mind capable
of searching out such truth.

We think God is against us
when He only wants to be close!

God respects principles and potentials
more than he respects present positions
of poor or prominent persons.

God, through our extended awareness,
can portray before our minds the universal
manifestation of Himself in a moment of time.

❧
Gold

He who only seeks on earth for wealth of gold denies
himself greatly in this world, and in the world to come,
he finds denial written above the gates of celestial gold.

❧
Good

The ideal social good is brotherhood;
the anti-social person is often just a "hood."

❧
Gossip

The gossip speaks his half-truths through false teeth.

If you close your talk shop, it will take some of the wear
and tear off of the gossip's tongue who feels a compulsion
to spread your lingual litter to every lawn in town.

The gossip leaves his mouth motor running in a close
place until he asphyxiates himself, his hearers,
or the object of his ill-intended attention.

Gossip, like the gopher, runs in one hole and comes out in
another, but he is always dragging his tale
in somebody's dirt!

William R. Jackson

The vulture and the gossip are carrion cousins.
They are always carrin' something that stinks.

The dog that wags his tail before he
bites is no worse than the gossip who
wags his tongue and smiles while he
bites you from behind.

If the busybodies, the tale bearers,
and the gossips were all hanged from high
scaffolds by the tips of their tongues,
their feet would still drag in the dirt.

The eager-eyed, open-eared scandal listener
is a sure bet for the gossip girls' "queen for a day."

The alligator kills with his tail
and so does the scandal monger.

Was the little bird who told you
so a mockingbird, a silly goose,
a dumb do-do, or just another old hen?

The person who is careless with the truth is an artist at
misrepresentation who can paint holes in the canvas
where no defect ever had been.

The gossip, like the echo, repeats on empty air the
things he heard another day of one who isn't there.

ॐ
Gratitude

Gratitude is the first debt we owe to heaven, whose
courts ring empty without earth's paean of praise!

Gratefulness is the coin of courtesy; and he is bankrupt
indeed who neglects to pay his debts of gratitude.

When beggars' boons are granted
the wise return with praise.

The glue of gratitude cements fragile friendships.

To ask a favor is pardonable, but ingratitude is not.

The mange of ingratitude leaves a bare spot
on man or beast.

Ingratitude, like the logger with ax and saw,
works in the shade of the tree it undercuts!

Ingratitude is the treason of the thankless heart.

Ingratitude bites the hand that blesses it
and licks its lips for more.

Gratitude is an attitude that tunes the human heart
to the vibrations of harmony divine.

Gratitude is the gateway to God, the door to gratuities,
and the most gracious gift that the grateful man
can give in return.

≈

Grave

The grave is probably one house you'll never live in!

≈

Greatness

Greatness would sink half out of sight if we could quit
our groveling; and the other half we could equal by
achievements of our own!

Greatness is often a matter of quality rather than size.

ॐ
Habit

Habit is repeated activity that becomes automatic;
accident, circumstance, or choice may begin it, but once
firmly fixed, the will may need divine assistance
to substitute a different action pattern.

Habit is the customary direction
we give to the expression of the
inner energy of universal vital force.

The steepest mountain you'll ever climb
is the side of the rut you're in!

Poor habits are as hard to strip off as adhesive
on a hairy hand.

From cobwebs to cables our habits grow;
and by indulgence repeated the strong are brought low.

As the dog's tail curls when the splints are off,
so our habits return when restraint is gone.

Reformation is often the serpent only shedding its skin;
bad habits persist until the nature is changed.

❧

Happiness

Happiness is an inner attitude
rather than outward circumstance.

A garden of small pleasures is more fragrant
than the desert of ingratitude.

The art of happiness is the fine balance found somewhere
between grateful awareness, increased achievement,
and adjusted desires.

❧

Haste

Haste and hurry are activity exceeding
the speed limits of efficiency.

❧

Hate

When everybody smells bad, try taking a bath yourself.

No man is duty bound to hate unless he wants to make
installment payments on his wounded pride.
Some debts are better left unpaid.

Forget the hateful things that hurt you;
there are other lives to live.

The man who hates, hurts himself,
and the man who hurts another, hates himself.

Hate is spawned by helplessness, and he is strongest who
can forget, forgive, and find a way of helpfulness.

Hate is indulged on some occasions and then
it cries its wares when uninvited.

We search for cause to hate the people we have wronged;
thus corrupted conscience calms itself.

Hate etches the lines of tension in the loveless face and
paints a portrait of dismay and gloom that hangs
foreboding in the gallery of the human heart.

We do not just have enemies; we make them,
or someone else does for us.

Neither love nor hate have foundations
always forged in facts. Fickle emotion
must be firmly held in hand.

It is safer to hold the puma's paw than the
hand of illicit love; a condemned conscience
of ten cancels love with hate.

The crabapple tree by a river of syrup
would still bear bitter fruit!

❧

Health

Poor fools would trade their health for riches
while rich ones would trade their wealth for health.

Health is the heritage of life
even as sickness is the door to death.

Resist the thought of ill health
before it is fully manifest in an ill body.

Keep the machinery of your mind a body well oiled with
exercise and the loose parts tightened with temperance.

If your wife is a widow, how can you advise her on how
to spend your insurance money?

Health lies in the happiness of the poor who rejoice as
though they were rich and in the temperance of the rich
who abstain as though they were poor.

❧

Helpfulness

It is better to divide than to lose everything.

The man who cannot give money can best
give something of himself: kind words, timely
knowledge, the liberality of love, and the
wealth of a willing heart.

Helpfulness invigorates the helper, and the helping hand
is strengthened for its own.

Happiness and helpfulness are Siamese twins; both of
them come when the other is called.

To inspire self-improvement, to teach self-help, and to
maintain self-respect is the truest charity.

The successful need encouragement like the ocean needs
rain; it's the man who almost made it
who needs helpfulness and praise.

To assist the wrongdoer is like pouring water in a
contaminated well.

When the cow gives steaks, she gives her life;
liberality in excess defeats itself.
Cows should give only their milk.

The breeze that fans the fire in excess blows out the light.

Experience has the softest hands, but the childless nurse
lacks sympathy when the labor pains begin.

A mother's knee is for comfort or for correction; in either case, a cooperative child is benefited by it.

We can only give what we have.
A pink sheep with a poodle trim still can't bark,
and a cat with a dog collar can't herd sheep.
It's what we are, not what we seem,
that determines the degree of our helpfulness.

A funeral procession stops at the grave,
but good influence does not.

We must help ourselves; knowing the
truth is good, but reading the label
on the bottle is no substitute
for taking the medicine.

~

Home

The horse knows his manger, the dog knows his corner,
the homing pigeon knows his perch, and happy is the
man who knows that home is the closest place
to heaven on this earth.

Home isn't so much a place as it is a relationship,
a confidence, and a condition. Home is where love
makes its dwelling.

Honesty

Honesty is an anchor, honor is a compass,
and integrity is a port; without these,
great ships go down in the storms at sea.

The longer you live without honesty, the longer
restitution's road grows; it is better not to travel
a road you would rather not retrace.

Hope

Hope is a lamp with faith the flame;
it makes fear's phantoms flee.

A hanging man's hope is in a breaking rope; for even a
rope doesn't hold much hope when you're hanging by
your neck and not by your hands.

Hope without foundation in fact or faith leaves only the
false bottom of delusion on which to stand.

Hope is man's steady star at night and
the rising sun of the day.

Hope is a banker in the business of loaning confidence
to the cautious and courage to cowards.

Hope should begin with the possible,
progress with industry to the probable,
and proceed to the achievement of the actual.

False hope is no friend to faith
and on occasion has destroyed it.

Hope is a fragrant, fragile flower around which the
"would-bees" buzz.

Fear is a nightmare of delusion,
but hope is a happy dream brought to mind.

Hope is Hercules holding up the world while
Atlas rubs his aching back.

Hope has calloused hands that labor while it waits.

Hope is a nightingale that
sings at every man's window.

Excessive hope is best counterbalanced by caution
but not capsized by fear.

The greatest poverty is hopelessness!

Hope must awaken the will to work and the resolution
to recover from reverses.

Hope, like bread, is the staff of life, but, alas
it's not always buttered!

༄

Humanity

Humanity is the family of God; and He loves no child
less, nor another more.

Femininity is the mother of humanity, the sister
of humanity, the daughter of humanity, the heart and
hope of humanity, and, on occasion, the headache of
humanity; still, masculinity declares that femininity
is the most attractive part of humanity.

There should be a "people shelter" in the Humane Society
for unfortunate humanity so often in "the doghouse."

Fortunately, humanity still bears some stamp of divinity.

༄

Humor

If you're looking for a good joke,
don't forget the looking glass.

~
Ideals

Ideals should be focused on the far
horizon where both earth and heaven
meet, but not so far or so high
as to be entirely "out of this world."

Idealism is the strength of
democracy; and statesmen become
politicians without it.

Ideals are the national treasure;
but materialism can corrode it away.

Ideals energize, vitalize, invigorate,
chart our courses, measure our values,
and test our methods and motives.

Our greatest national debt is our allegiance to our
national ideals of individual initiative, integrity, faith,
freedom, religion, and service!

ॐ
Ideas

Practical ideas are the seedlings of thought,
the solutions to problems, the answers
to questions, and the reward for the effort
of an industrious, imaginative mind.

Ideas have legs! Right ideas and strong
ones will walk with you through life,
help you climb your mountains,
support you when the road seems long,
and carry you to the end of the day;
for good ideas have strong legs.

ॐ
Imagination

Imagination is constructive, obstructive,
or destructive, depending upon its control
and direction.

Imagination is the ability to recall vividly the old images;
to create new mental concepts that are visible in the
mind's eye, or combinations of creative imagery; and to
conceive and construct from the recalled material of past
experience new forms, new methods, new conditions,
and new pictorial thoughts as subjective embodiments
as yet unmanifest.

❧

Imitation

It is easier to smear the carbon copy than the original.

Imitation is instinctive; however, there is seldom much
left to imitate but imitators.

To initiate or imitate, to be the voice or the echo,
that's the question.

It is hard to copyright a counterfeit; and it is equally
difficult to borrow individuality or distinction.

❧

Immortality

Christianity is the proof of immortality,
and immortality is the hope of Christianity.

When the dust of mortality is blown afar,
the door of immortality will be standing ajar.

Immortality learns to lisp its lessons of eternal life while
still on earth; but it matriculates forever on the campus
of Celestial Completion.

Christianity is a correspondence course;
but immortality is the diploma on graduation day.

Immortality is an unending symphony of
universal harmony in heaven; and it is
one concert for which all mortals,
musicians or not, should make
immediate reservations.

ॐ

Impatience

Impatience is a half-broke horse that wants to go
before it knows how, where, or even why.

Patience, not impatience, is the soil in which
the seeds of development grow.

Man frets at time and pulls his half-grown
roots of labor out of the soil of progress
to see if they are as stunted as he knows
they will be after he is done.

The man who can pin impatience's shoulders
on the mat will rise to wrestle more successfully
in his conquest of favorable fortune.

Impatience bears a brood of brats
called Restless, Resentful, Remorseful,
Rebellion, and Ruin.

❧

Impossibility

Impossibility is an unthinkable word
that challenges divine creativity
and stirs the blood of
courageous men to action.

Unbelief is a restless beast, self-chained to the
pole of impossibility.

❧

Improvement

Self-contemplation more readily
inspires discouragement than
improvement; for the lesser must
always behold the better for a
pattern of progress.

He who improves must often improvise.

❧

Impulse

How can we blame an action that from
unthinking impulse sprang?

ॐ
Inattention

Inattention puts water in the gas tank, gas in the radiator,
oil in the window washer, and a traffic hazard
under the steering wheel.

ॐ
Incentive

Individual incentive is the seedling of success; actual
achievement is the harvest brought home through
persistence and labor.

ॐ
Indifference

Indifference is the difference
between industry and insolvency!

The man who sits in the bleachers doesn't banquet with
the champions; activity has its rewards.

ॐ
Industry

The escalator is the only place it isn't necessary to keep
on climbing; and even that has been done by people who
are in a hurry or who have the habit.

&

Infidelity

Infidelity is willful nearsightedness
where self in grotesque disproportion
obstructs a view of God.

Infidelity blossoms in rebellion and is the fruit of
disobedience; its skepticism is self-deception for
self-justification because of self-inflation and
self-indulgence, however expressed.

There is the possibility of some degree of sincerity
in the self-delusion of superficial and
incompetent atheism;
and on it the hope of conversion rests.

The minister who undermines the faith he professes
and the congregation he serves is by example and
argument a greater infidel than the skeptic
who with lesser light still questions "why."

The unbroken silence of the tomb,
and the cold shadow of death,
have a way of making the truth eclipse error
and the atheist pass into forgetfulness
and oblivion.

~

Influence

The consequence of good or evil deeds
can never be measured in time or by
the measuring rod
of the mortal mind.

My influence is my shadow, line for line;
the fault for what it blights or
blesses, too, is mine.

If a lifetime of evil influence could be
buried in the grave, God knows how many
by its absence it might save.

~

Ingrate

The ungrateful are the unworthy, and nothing
grates more greatly than an ingrate!

~

Initiative

Initiate—don't hesitate; to start something
and even fail is better than to start nothing
and succeed gloriously.

Initiative is the drive for beginning something,
the spirit of conquest, and the self-starter for action.
What it begins should be the product of creative
imagination, balanced by judgment,
sustained by courage, and directed
to some worthwhile end.

Initiative is active aptitude!

෧

Insults

Few insults are given if few are expected; and fewer
will be forthcoming if the first is rejected!

If a man acts uncomprehending,
it is difficult to know if you have successfully
insulted him or not; herein feigned stupidity is
wiser than the genuine stupidity
of taking offense too easily.

෧

Intemperance

A man might better hope to drink the ocean dry
than to satisfy intemperance on the sly.

ॐ
Interest

Interest precedes advancement
as reward proceeds from work; and there is no hope
of a harvest even in good soil where interest
and attention have not been sown.

Success does not come so much to us
at first as from us; for the seeds of
interest and intention must be planted
in the soil first of the inner self
from which all things grow.

Jealousy

Jealousy is the fog and ferment of the disordered mind.

Jealousy knows no appeasement, for it takes concessions as confession to all its wild imaginings.

Jealousy is a bloated spider full of venom that weaves its web of suspicion and feeds with equal greed on fact or fantasy.

Love is expansive; jealousy is not. Jealousy is constriction, restriction, and contraction; selfishness is a python that chokes itself to death.

Self-love cries its jealous wares so loudly in the marketplace that true love hides its face, and strangers fear to buy where tolerance and reason are scarcely heard above the din of distraught passion.

The jealous are never alone. They make bedfellows of Doubt, Distrust, Suspicion, Apprehension, and Fear.

The jealous distrust each passerby and scare themselves
more than others by their constant barking;
braver dogs bark less and bite only when necessary.

Let not the toothless snarling of old dogs turn you from
your path; they are angry not so much at your ambition
as at the lack of their own.

Jealousy proves a want of love and seeks a cause for hate;
yet by its vain imaginings, it suffers every fate.

If imagined inferiority could find a true security, then
jealous passion's flame would smolder for want of air.

Jealousy is a glass that magnifies the trifles that it
remotely sees, while it blurs the sturdier virtues closer by.

The green eyes of jealousy are often blind; they seek for
faults, but virtues seldom find.

Jealousy can see with jaundiced eye,
deception in each breeze that passes by.

☙

Jobs

No bear trap should grip a grizzly's leg more fiercely
than purpose should bear down on opportunity;
hold your job down and dig yourself in with efficiency,
loyalty, application, and learning.

A job isn't security; it is opportunity.

Your job is your stage; and it is your part to act
successfully the character part assigned to you.

☙

Joke

He jests best who jests with the quick witted;
for even as beauty is in the eye of the beholder,
so humor is more in the ear of the listener
than in the tale told.

☙

Judgment

The scales of judgment weigh not deeds alone,
but every thought within the human heart.

Suspend thy judgment until all the facts are in;
for to censure without knowledge is injustice
wearing the robes of ignorance.

Good judgment hath ample ears for careful listening,
a sound mind to consider wisely, an unbiased will
to decide fairly, and kind lips to pronounce
its decrees with gentleness.

Additional evidence, not want of judgment, causes the
discerning man to change his mind.

Question your own judgment with caution
when desire is overly strong, or when ambition,
like a short-reined horse, paws the earth and
mouths its bit with flashing eye.

ॐ
Justice

How impartial is the Mother Earth
in the benefits she renders unto all!

Patient justice with its sturdy legs will sooner or later
catch up with crime, although the crooked legs of evil are
sometimes longer and more skilled in running.

Justice when withheld too long
is injustice practiced by the strong.

Justice is the hope of the just
and the dread of wrongdoers.

The man who dispenses justice
has courage to demand it for himself.

Justice feared is judgment avoided;
but justice loved is wisdom rewarded.

To give justice or receive it—which is best?
Both, for justice is a virtue doubly blessed!

Kindness

Kindness is the only bootstrap by which a man
may lift himself without finding someone
who wants to trip him up.

The hard-surfaced, porcelain-white refrigerator
saints who quick-freeze all offered friendships
and keep the door securely closed on
their dehydrated virtues may find themselves
defrosted somewhere other than in heaven.

Kindness at least will listen when it can do no more.

Better one act of thoughtful kindness carved in the
memory of a friend than a marble shaft with your
forgotten name chiseled on it.

Kindness without fanfare is more impressive
and is accepted with the greatest appreciation
because its motives seem to be the most sincere.

ᔧ
Kinship

It is not so much blood ties, nationality,
knowledge, or position, but fellow
feeling and the bonds of
kindness that make all men one.

ᔧ
Kiss

Lips cautiously say with kisses
what the heart lacks courage to tell.

A kiss may tell a thousand things
or still conceal the same; for a kiss is
what the heart reveals as the lips
spell out its name.

A reserved smile on fresh-kissed lips
may be as deadly as the cobra's grin.

No more can salt quench thirst
than can one kiss suffice without another
and still another; for the kiss that satisfied
arouses feelings that are not.

William R. Jackson

To kiss the dew of innocence from unkissed lips
is to taste the dew of heaven bejeweled
on the petals of a soft, white rose.

≈

Knowledge

If desire opens the door wide enough, knowledge will
move in, bookshelves and all, and it may even be said in
the future that "wisdom once lived here."

❧
Laughter

The man who can't laugh with others
has been too long in the shadow
of his own company
and too little in the light.

Laughter penetrates the dried
harness leather of a dour face,
like saddle soap and oil, and gives the smiling
flexibility of a pair of new moccasins.

A man's nature is revealed by the quality,
the quantity, and the propriety of his
laughter, even as the shrill,
cowardly cry of the carrion-eating
hyena betrays his identity by his
laughter in the shadows.

To laugh with someone is fellowship; to laugh at
someone is folly; and laughter always lacks humor
when it is at your own expense.

William R. Jackson

Humanity takes great stock in the therapy of laughter,
but few care to be the laughingstock that cures
the ailments of laughing humanity.

The superior laugh of arrogance, pride,
or ill intent is a broken, two-edged sword
that in time will cut the hand of him
who wields it without mercy.

The echo of laughter voices the empty walls of the soul,
or speaks its inner warmth and fullness.

The unguarded laugh reveals readily
what men and women have carefully covered
with a camouflage of words and works.

The mad laughter of folly, the empty
laughter of ignorance, the sinister laughter
of evil, the bitter laughter of disillusionment,
the cold laughter of hate, the determined
laughter of purpose, the carefree laughter
of little children, the loving laughter of
comradeship, and the holy laughter of
inner joy each speaks its mind unerringly
without the voice of words!

If laughter came in bottles and every pill
were free, some folks would do without
them and pay for severity.

Some people who have tried both say it's much easier to
laugh at a bad joke than to hang from a good rope!

❧

Law

The weaker the law of inner constraint,
the greater the volume of legal restraint; and the
self-disciplined will seldom need costly correction.

In the reward of a law observed is greater strength
than in the punishment of its infraction; for virtue
rewarded is a sturdier tree than unwilling virtue
however reinforced by restraint.

❧

Lawyers

Geese who cannot agree pluck each other's feathers
to line the lawyers' nests.

❧

Learning

When school is out,
students choose their own books and teachers.

Learning is life, not enforced schooling,
and those who learn willingly learn best.

Learning is richer than riches and stronger
than strength; it extends time by making it more
productive and life by making it more meaningful.

~

Lectures

The married man has arranged for a lifelong lectureship
in the college of his choice where he often receives the
"third degree" without graduation or honors.

~

Leisure

Leisure time can mean anything from dull inactivity to
opportunity for purposeful self-employment.

~

Letters

Who knows but that a letter sealed with love
and penned with care may by its invisible words
and overtones a deeper message bear.

~

Liberty

Liberty is a glad word ringing like the pealing of a bell;
and liberty is a sad word that brave men and women in
battle bled for where they fell.

ॐ
Library

A library is a silent mausoleum where the dehydrated
wisdom of the past is preserved in varicolored,
clothbound caskets, row on row, where ancient treasure
without lock or key awaits the explorer who has
courage for such grave digging.

ॐ
Life

Life is but one day; in the morning we call it tomorrow,
at noon we call it today, but in the evening we call it
yesterday, and try to recall it again.

Life is action, time is its dimension,
and immortality is its reward.

He who lives too fast to savor life seems not to have
lived too long; but he who lives most fully adds
extra stanzas to his once-heard song.

The life is long enough that fully works out
the purposes for which that life was born.

Life, like the eagle's flight, seems to float without sense
of time, space, or motion; and like a Pacific sunset
it seems to pause for reflection, then is swallowed
by death's restless ocean.

Most lives are but a river of limited consciousness that fills its own banks but waters no arid lands along its shores; and it leaves no monuments of cities, vineyards, or fruitful harvests in remembrance that it passed this way or shared itself in its journey to the vast unknown.

The love of life is a beautiful thing; it is the infinite within the finite that senses the beauty of the finite with infinite sensitivity and intuitive appreciation.

☙

Light

The moon lights up the night better than a thousand sightless eyes; so an illuminated man reflects his inner wisdom among the multitudes with lesser stars for light.

Let the light of truth direct your path, the lamp of reason guard your steps, and the candle of courage give you confidence; for he is not alone who walks in light.

☙

Listeners

Let the wheat of wisdom always outweigh the chaff of your untested self-opinions lest the listening harvesters find they have labored half the day to find a kernel or two of doubtful grain.

֎

Listening

Listening is the sweetest eloquence
that wisdom ever hears.

֎

Love

The absence of the unity of cohesive love
is disintegration in all things.

Love is a rope so strong that nothing on earth need break
it; for its strands are kindness, constancy, and care, and it
is no stronger than the hearts that make it; and neglect,
not use, will make it show the most wear.

Love is life's fundamental necessity; without it, emotions
lose their purpose and, like Noah's dove, can find no solid
place to rest their feet.

Unselfishness and love are fraternal friends and even
twins; but drab selfishness and filial doubt no affinity of
love or oneness ever wins.

He who claims God as his Father must by necessity treat
the rest of humanity as his brothers!

Love does not complain of the child's crippled feet
but looks rather at how the crutches may be made
more comfortable or the journey happier.

Love is a song that has a harmony and uplift all its own;
and happy is the man who learns to sing it with others,
for love's Great Composer intended it not for solos as
much as for ensembles.

Each life is a minstrel outside the castle walls of every
other soul, and only the song of love will open the
windows and unbar the iron gates.

Hate can pulverize opposition like crushed ice, but only
the warmth of understanding and love can melt it away.

The man who rules his reflexes will not ruin his
reflections or rue his reactions half so much.

Even love should have its vacations, for afterwards,
its treasures shine brighter in the new perspective
that distance and time renewed.

Love with its wings clipped is no longer love; for love
enforced is fractured love, and if the force used to retain it
had been used to gain it, it would not exist at all.

In the test of enduring love, character,
not passion, charm, emotion, or beauty,
should tip the scales of attraction.

Let thy life be like the cool, green ivy that, spreading over
stone and weathered windowsill, hides well the faults of
all it clings to for support.

≈

Loyalty

There can be no treachery or double-dealing hate
in a loyalty that's worthy of the name.

Loyal service is royal service; for the loyal are the royal
rulers in the kingdom of faithful service. Trustworthiness
is their crown and dependability their golden throne.

Distrust makes for disloyalty and disloyalty for distrust;
but loyalty is the first requirement for the commitment of
responsibility and the last quality to be sacrificed in the
reduction of forces.

Mix equal parts of faithfulness, unselfishness,
trustworthiness, steadfastness, dependability, confidence,
courage, cooperation, common purpose, and uncommon
love and you can whip up a batch of loyalty that will
stand the long stretch like rubber and stick together
like silicone cement.

122

Luck

Don't count good fortune out,
even though you don't count it first.

The unlucky are the unlikely
because they are the unreliable.

It takes more than good luck to build skyscrapers, perfect
inventions, write classics, paint masterpieces, or attain
your purposes in life; but good fortune and even chance
have been known to turn the tide in favor of success.

Lay such an attractive foundation of plans, purposes,
and persistent progress that even good luck will
want to rent office space where you live.

When good luck seems to leave for the moment,
remember that the good Lord hasn't.

Marriage

In a good marriage, each is a mirror that reflects
the best in the other without trying to break
what it can't see through.

The man who opens his mouth in proposal
should keep it closed after the
wedding. You asked for it.

The fiercest predator of all the wild kingdom
is a woman in search of a mate;
the man-eating tiger runs a close second
but with nobler intentions.

Divorce can't cure what cussedness
causes; let the woman who makes her
own bedlam sleep in it.

The chains do not rattle too loudly in marriage
if the man follows his wife quietly.

The man who listens to a wedding march
must continue to walk that narrow aisle
and face the music for the rest of his natural life;
and the ten dollars he so generously paid the minister
was only the down payment on an endless
installment plan more properly called the
"marriage mortgage."

Many a little tail is wagging a big dog.

~

Medicine

There are no greater doctors than Faith, Hope, and Love;
they cure more sickness by their practice than all the
patent medicines in the world.

~

Memory

Any ill-intended deed is a cadaver that
should be wrapped in a shroud of love and
buried in a casket of forgiveness in the
cemetery of forgetfulness with no headstone
to memorialize its forgotten resting place.

The man who would purchase a good
memory must keep his installment accounts
current by paying attention.

Women and elephants are very much
alike except that elephants are not
as flighty and seem to remember
their grudges almost as long.

The man with a phenomenal memory
observes more details and relationships
in what he sees and hears,
and with greater intent to recall
them accurately.

A good memory depends upon associating
new things with the old by observing
the similarities and differences.

Meaningful classification of knowledge, and confidence
in memory's ability to automatically recall it, is the
foundation of meaningful learning.

The man who would increase the efficiency of his
memory must commend it and not condemn it;
for self-confidence, not criticism, encourages efficiency.

&

Misfits

Too many draft horses are being groomed for the races
while too many potential racers are hitched
to monotony's plow.

❧
Mistakes

To make mistakes is evidence of ambition and application,
with action just one jump ahead of judgment.

Mistakes are a part of the labor and construction costs
of building profitable experience.

The number of your mistakes may measure the extent
of your determined activity rather than the degree
of your stupidity.

Your witness to weakness is unwelcome by the wise,
for they know that men identify
with the objects of their awareness.

Dismantle your mistakes and analyze each part in the
light of the basic laws of right thinking; then profit by
them, but never become emotionally fascinated or
self-hypnotized by any miserable mistake. Forget it.

Unchain past errors from your feet;
it's best for progress or retreat!

❧
Moderation

Self-control is the criterion, and moderation the mandate,
for the man who would be an anchor, not just flotsam and
jetsam in the sea of survival.

~

Money

Wealth comes to the
enlightened like rivers flow
down to the sea.

The fact of wealth always follows
after the subjective feeling of
wealth. Prosperity is the projected
product of the inner security,
abundance, and possession of
divine substance and supply.

The God who made a million
stars and more can help a man
make a million dollars, especially
if he needs a million dollars
like the night needs a million stars.

All ill-gotten money is fools' gold!

The love of money may be the
root of all evil, but money itself is a
root from whose branches most
material and many spiritual
blessings spring.

The materialist believes that we were
not put here to make friends or enemies,
but simply to make money. The humanist
believes that we were put here not to
make money or enemies, but to make friends.
The philanthropist believes that we
were put here to make money so we can
help both our friends and our
enemies. The idealist believes that we
were put here to make friends if possible,
to make enemies if necessary,
to make money when needed,
but above all, to make it to heaven
and to help our enemies and friends
to make it, too.

Money is a linguist who can say,
"Goodbye, now!" in every known
language and under every conceivable
circumstance in the world; and it has been known
to leave without bothering to say, "Goodbye."

❧

Moods

Moods are wonderful if you have the
optimistic, positive, consistent kind!

❧
Nature

Nature is the hand of God
reaching out of the sleeve of
Divine Immensity to caress you
as you pass Him by unnoticed.

All nature is but the garment
of God, and those who lean
hard against God's garments
can feel the heartbeat of the Divine.

Nature both conceals and reveals
God to the minds of men;
those who look long and
lovingly will find Him everywhere.

Nature is a flower blooming on
the banks of the time–space
continuum; but God, the Divine
Gardener, is standing always nearby.
All nature is God's temple.

The sunsets are His stained-glass windows;
the sky is the temple's blue-vaulted dome;
the harmony of nature, from the thunder to the bird's
song, is His organ; and all rocks, stones, or resting places
everywhere are His benches. The congregation is
composed of all the listening world; the only collection
that the angel ushers take is the tribute of our love
and praise as they share our sacrament of service
as we rise to labor in the same spirit
that we paused to worship and to pray.

In the secret, dark, and hidden places of nature,
unsullied even by the thoughts of man,
we sense the God of nature lingering near
in the unbroken solitude.

❧

Needs

Contentment is not indulged abundance,
but happy adjustment tempered with the progress
of continuous creative activity.

Man's greatest need in life is not more or less
of any material thing; his greatest need is for a truer sense
of direction, wiser evaluation, and the cooperative
enthusiasm of unselfish love that makes life
more meaningful and adds the zest of
purpose well directed.

ॐ
Noise

Thunder is nature's advertising that tells
where the lightning struck.

It is not the roar of the cannon but the shot that kills;
only occasionally is noise effective or fatal.

Noise is disagreeable sound in excess;
and any incessant noise is naturally an annoyance
of noisome nature.

ॐ
Now

The past is gone;
the future may or may not come;
our only time to live, to learn, to love, or to labor
is wrapped up in that fleeting thing called "now!"

The question is not why, or where, or even how;
but all the past or hoped-for future is in the present,
here and now!

Obedience

Obedience should be predicated
on cooperative confidence, not on
conditioned compliance alone;
for obedience is consistent with
liberty only when it is voluntary,
intelligent, and ultimately beneficial.

Experience quickly teaches wisdom to obey;
but folly never learns the difference
between the giving that increases
and the withholding that costs more.

Obligation

Mankind lives in a world of intricate, intermeshed
obligations and reciprocal responsibilities to countless
individuals, institutions, and instrumentalities;
when obligation is neglected, all parts suffer.

❧
Observation

To observe wisely is to avoid the obvious
and investigate the intriguing.

❧
Obstacles

Men with indomitable wills
seldom find insurmountable obstacles.

❧
Occupation

No man should be occupied with less than that which
interests him most and for which God has given him
the greatest gifts of usefulness.

❧
Ocean

The salty, seaweed-swaying, swelling,
shore-caressing ocean speaks of preserving power;
the storm-tossed, wave-crested, surging ocean is
suggestive of misdirected, dynamic, destructive power;
but the calm, far-reaching sea, reflecting the lights of the
setting sun, is symbolic of the powers of progress, peace,
and the immensity of the divine reserve and potential
available to all voyaging mankind.

William R. Jackson

☙

Old Age

Tranquility fosters longevity
and happiness is the harbinger of health.

Man's age is not measured so much
from the latitude of his years as by his attitudes,
his aspirations, and his fears!

What the mind accepts, the body reflects.

Negative suggestion accepted, and
the senility of courage, and faith grown
weary, produce in the body the seed
pictures planted in the soil of the mind.

Old age is a floating raft in a stagnant mill pond
for people who drifted out of the main current
and have lost their pole and their push,
or their oars and their ambitions.

The premature appearance of the aging
process is the result of the subjective
acceptance of the feelings and mental
pictures of the characteristics of age.
Inner visioning is the blueprint
for the continuous destructive
reconstruction of our body cells.

The activities, the habits, the attitudes,
the ideals, the aspirations, the ambitions,
the habitual feelings, and the self-image of youthfulness
hold back the tide of unwelcome decrepitude.

The thought looms of morbidity
produce the fabric of old age and
lay out our measured shroud when
we should be trading in our caskets
for the consecrated commitment to
perennial youth and happiness.

Positive thoughts, progress,
and the practice of perpetual-youth picturization
produce the appearance and vigor of youth;
pessimism promotes only retrogression
and unwanted decadence of body and mind.

To sleep well and nap occasionally;
to eat less and more simply;
to worry little and love much;
to live without tension, competition,
irritation, criticism, or hostility;
to have faith in God and in humanity;
to have contentment, security, tranquility,
calmness, confidence, and serenity;
to practice moderation, relaxation, and exercise,
will help one live better
and much, much longer.

William R. Jackson

❧

Opportunity

Opportunity is a golden moment, awakened by
awareness, selected with discernment,
set in the brooch of preparedness, cut and shaped by
man's purpose, purchased by resolution and denial,
and worn in the honor of attainment.

Opportunity means nothing to a tiger without teeth!

Opportunities have their seasons;
but be ready to plant in the spring,
hoe in the summer, and harvest in the fall.

Opportunity may be the conquest of adversity
as well as the smile of good fortune.

The magnetism of optimism and the
radiance of positive thinking attract
opportunities, goodwill, and good fortune
like moths are attracted to the brightest light.

Some men simply wait for opportunity
and grasp it gratefully if it comes, while others prepare
for it but fail to recognize or claim it as their own;
but the determined go out to seek it, to make it,
to master it, and to mold the half opportunities
into whole achievements.

Foresight and insight rather than hindsight
are the binoculars for spotting an opportunity
while it is still coming our way.

Inventory your potentials
and you will discover your opportunities.

The opportunity to get something
is never as ultimately satisfying as the
opportunity to give something; however,
the ideal opportunity combines
exceptional service with ultimate rewards.

∂

Opposition

It is much better to have opposition
than to have the habit of opposing.

∂

Optimism

Constructive optimism is an observatory
built on the rock promontory of faith, hope, and love.

Tomorrow, tomorrow! This is the
optimist's land; and strangely enough,
it bears the birthmarks of its imaged
expectations when it comes.

Optimism knows there is more danger in pessimism
than in positivism and wisely chooses the determining
attitude that produces the happiest consequences.

It is folly, not optimism, to expect changes without
causes, rewards without effort, or harvest without
plowing and planting!

Optimism is a suit that shines brightest
where it is worn the most: the knees of the pants
may be shiny from persistent crawling toward its goal,
or from sincere praying; but whatever the point of
encounter, optimism shines best where hardest pressed!

෬

Oratory

The minister's sermon is most eloquent
to those he has visited during the week.

෬

Organization

Organization is the fruit of mutually beneficial
but modified independence.

The flame of liberty needs the lantern of discipline, the
glass chimney of expression, and the wick and the oil of
cooperative energy and organization.

ༀ

Originality

Originality epitomizes truth and finds the straightest
route to the throne room of the heart.

The original thinker can find within himself life's
important questions and, by continuing his quest, can also
find the faculty within that channels the answer through
him from the fountain of infinite wisdom
and intuitive knowledge.

The great mind will strike across the fields of thought
and leave the beaten path of parroted, verbal phrases
behind. For courage, not caution; independence,
not servitude; creativity, not compliance, are the
blessed eccentricities of those who think for
themselves and thus for all who follow.

ༀ

Orphan

He is an orphan indeed
whose life purposes are not sired
by just ambition, nurtured by
fervent desire, schooled in the creed
of service, and accepted in the
household of humanity.

Pardon

Only goodness and greatness find it easy to give
and to forgive, to be gracious in pardon,
and humble in the position of power.

Passion

From the soil of directed passion
the virtues of creativity, good, and true greatness arise.

Passion without direction is a hungry horse, with blinders
on his bridle but no reins, looking for greener pastures
while unmindful of the dangers on either side.

Patience

It is wiser to stand still than to run in the wrong direction.

Impatience frightens the pigeons
by scattering the grain too fast.

Patient

The doctor needs the patient's purse
as badly as the patient needs the doctor's
pills, or worse!

Patriotism

Too often, vested interests and
political expediency post patriotism
signs on the closed-door conferences
of self-interest.

Patriotism, which is love, loyalty,
and allegiance to one's country,
does not necessitate racial prejudice,
imagined superiority, or international
snobbery; and it respects the same
quality of patriotism in the loyal citizen
of another country.

Payment

From expected remuneration to
unexpected retribution, compensation is
motivation, punishment, and reward.

William R. Jackson

❧

Penmanship

Our faces are the pad;
our thoughts the shorthand of the mind;
and time is the scribe that traces on
our faces the map of what
we seek and find.

The ink that flows from inspired pens
will rule the world long after the
blood spilled by the rusted swords
of war has disappeared.

❧

Perseverance

The man who has perseverance has
the treasure map for the
desert of adversity.

It's not the beginning that counts
as much as how and where we end.

Stop signs and caution lights are
necessary for traffic
regulation, but perseverance
adjusts to the traffic flow and
keeps on keeping on!

Persistence

Persistence is a priceless possession;
fortitude is a fortune that the
faint-hearted forever forfeit.

Are you finished, or are you a finisher?
Persistence wins the day.

Are you a booer, a doer,
or a stop-before-you-are-through-er?
Whatever you do, be persistent.

The teeth of tenacity will rip
the fabric of adversity
and reveal the rewards
of persistence.

Personality

Your personality, like an umbrella,
is most effective when it opens up.

Personality is the gift wrapping
around the product called "you."
Do you have the right kind of product
in an attractive wrapper?

William R. Jackson

❧

Perspective

Even happiness carries a cup
of care in its withered hand;
but it rejoices that the cup is so small
that half a hand can bear it
while the other hand works gladly
to share its measure of joy.

❧

Pessimism

The pessimist is already blaming circumstances
for his expected defeat.

The pessimistic, failure-conscious man
sees a dark world where even
a little bright-colored success
would seem entirely out of place.

Not many pessimists sit at the head table
in the banquet of champions.

The pessimists do more than
their share of talking, because
the optimists are too busy building
better things than to be bothered
with bickering or the blues.

Pessimism and positiveness
both begin with the letter "p";
but you never hear pessimism speak positively
of peace, plenty, pleasure, purpose,
progress, prosperity, philanthropy,
promotion, providence, promises,
possessions, prayer, purity,
patience, perfection, permanence,
power, pluck, persistence,
proficiency, praise, or patriotism.
It just looks like there are a lot of good things
that pessimism doesn't know about!

∂

Philosophy

Philosophy, if forged from living truth, will never lead
away from God, Who is the way, the truth, and the life!

∂

Pictography

Mental pictography is the faith form
or the master mold into which desire and will
pour the free energy of life's creative forces.

In back of the detailed envisioning of achieving faith
must be the invincible purpose that the subjective
desire must become an objective fact.

William R. Jackson

Successful manifestation of things
hoped for depends upon visually
"playing house" in the new and
expected environment with as vivid
an imagination, and feeling of
ownership, as actual and grateful
present possession would make you feel.

☙

Poetry

Life would be all prose if it were not for poetry,
and "vice-worser!"

Poetry is an illuminated viewpoint that brings out
the hidden beauty to burnish the exterior of the ordinary.

Poetry, like beauty, is as much in the perception
of the viewer and the listener as it is in the
manifest form; and it rises from an intuitive
rearrangement of the commonplace into
an expression of the universal harmony and
rhythm of the inner essence of life's vital forces.

☙

Politician

Some politicians find it hard to speak standing
because they are usually lying!

Positive Thinking

The night brings out the owls,
and the day, the birds that sing.

Success is a positive mental attitude
in perpetual motion.

Positive thinking is an inner light;
you grow in its glow as you come and go.

The positive attitude expressed in
genuine gratitude brings the mind and
heart quickly into harmony and
communion with God in Whom all
positive virtues reside.

Possession

The possession of wealth
often makes men more miserable than the lack of it;
but the poor would gladly exchange brands of misery
on the first of every month.

The conceited man is self-possessed,
the selfish man is greed-possessed,
and the man who loves to possess possessions
is by possession's chains possessed.

William R. Jackson

๏ฝ
Poverty

You do not cure poverty by picturing it,
resenting it, or fighting it; you
replace its negative feelings
subjectively with positive feelings
based on universal abundance, and you
begin mentally to picture circumstances
not as they are but as you truly
want them to be. Then the fact of
abundance follows
the feeling of abundance.

Poverty as a state is not admirable,
although a willingness to put first things first is.

Forget your poverty.
It may be a present reality, but it became so,
or continued so, because of a subjective state of mind
where the facts of poverty were pictured vividly
and the feeling and identity of poverty
were accepted in the mind.

The preventive poverty that curbs opportunity,
forestalls education, undermines self-confidence,
discourages self-development, thwarts philanthropic
expressions of love, and makes possible achievement
improbable is of doubtful value.

❧
Practicality

The man who fishes in the water, not in the sky, usually
catches fish and still sees the sky reflected from above.

Some men stir up more noise, dust, and arm action
than an airplane propeller, but they never take off
in the dust storm they blow up!

❧
Praise

The employer is not wise who thinks money will take the
place of appreciation, or that appreciation alone will take
the place of money. Most men work for both!

❧
Preachers

The minister who does his parish calling by car
is a sole saver either way you look at it.

Virility, manhood, and a sense of mission
are ministerial prerequisites.

Preparation precedes inspiration, adaptation,
and interpretation; and it should include
calloused hands and calloused knees,
but never a calloused heart.

❧

The Presence of God

The grateful, the creative, and the confident
have a standing invitation in the presence of God.

❧

Pride

The man who looks down his nose in contempt
is asking to have his chin lifted.

❧

Prisoners

Oh, voice of my heart, from out of the
infinite stillness now calling, why should
disquietude rattle its chains of bondage or
fear the night shadows falling?

Men build prisons of self-limitation and pace the
narrow cells complaining for want of freedom.

❧

Problems

Our problems indicate some ability to comprehend
and solve them. Where there is little capacity for
problem solving, there is limited awareness.

It is better to meditate on truth than to combat error,
to concentrate on solutions rather than lament
about problems.

༔

Progress

The older the habit of failure grows,
the farther its hopes and its hairline recede;
but this is progress in reverse.

The instinctive purpose of all life on earth
is growth, development, and progress in
every area of being: body, mind, spirit,
and circle of social influence.

No man breathes earth's air in vain who
brings a great thought into focus,
and by it raises the IQ of humanity and lays a
foundation for the progress of posterity.

To attain your desires, let your goals be clear,
your faith expectant, your gratitude unceasing,
your purpose unfailing, your actions efficient,
and your progress unremitting.

Obstacles are a challenge to the resolute;
they seem to demand a pledge or proof of our persistence
and a demonstration of determined progress.

The wheels of universal cause grind on,
and yesterday lies mangled in the rutted road.
Today still proudly sits in the driver's seat
unaware that tomorrow it, too, shall die;
and that shining, beckoning angel, the future,
soon shall, in its turn, try a hand at shaping
destiny; but growing feeble with unending
labor, it shall come to lie broken with all our
yesterdays in the littered road of time and progress.

❧

Propaganda

Propaganda, the indoctrination of distortion,
would not stand up without the props of prejudice,
deception, and human gullibility.

❧

Prosperity

Fortune favors faith;
and prosperity is the possession of the prudent.

Fortune is a fickle maid
whose constancy is based on the conquest of courage
and the coercion of insistent possession.

Prosperity flees from the fearful;
but achievement associates with the audacious.

Miss Fortune is a Cinderella
without the magic wand of faith, fancy, or fortitude.
Miss Chance, Miss Stake, and Miss Management
are her ugly sisters.

Have something useful, creative, and ready at hand
to exchange for the prosperity overtures
that the magnetism of faith will attract to you.

Success should come more by creative than by
competitive effort and without raising the blood pressure
to the point that it threatens the enjoyment of it.

Individual prosperity is relative to the
practical provision, by mass production,
of the present needs of the people and must
be in line with progress and the desire of all
men for their own increase and completeness.

ॐ

Provision

When the calf is born the milk increases!

ॐ

Public Speaking

A speaker must digest a lot of print mentally in private
before he can sprint verbally in public.

154

Nowhere should a man try harder to make both ends
meet than in the middle of a speech!

Do not talk in your sleep or talk your audience to sleep;
for in either case there is no one listening to tell you how
little you said or to ask why it took so long.

❧

Punishment

The rod of correction is safe in the hand of love.

There is no bed as hard as an undeserved one.

❧

Purpose

If you really want the moon,
why not check out the possibilities of the space program.

Are you a raft caught in the current without a pole to
push with, or are you a great steamship breasting the
waves and bringing your ship into harbor?

Keep your objectives noble and your purpose high;
for there's a lot less traffic on the "through route."

Constancy of purpose is the crown of achievement,
and only those wear it who are subject
to their own sovereignty.

Qualifications

It is better for the moment to have
a small income than to have a small
personality; for the man who
improves himself soon improves
his position. Quality is the
best qualification.

The man who improves himself
improves his chances, and
opportunity loves
to be courted with a
firm and knowing hand.

No matter how good the quality or
how great our potential, corn unplanted
cannot grow; and money
is of little worth unless put
into circulation.

❧

Quality

Do not condemn the wave because it is
not as big as the ocean; and be glad
that even little men carry in some degree
the qualities and attributes of God.

Let the man who speaks in superlatives
keep an eye more to quality than to
quantity, which is more obvious.

❧

Quarrels

Those who win arguments lose friends;
and those who quarrel find little to salvage
in the broken fragments of desecrated friendship.

To company constantly with a quarrelsome
person is as fraught with danger as
playing Russian roulette
with all the chambers loaded!

Quarrels arise from terminology misunderstood,
variant viewpoints, insufficient information, and faulty
reasoning; but above all from a condition of inner
dissatisfaction with one's self for which
we know no remedy but distraction
through the discomfort of others.

A quarrel is the stench arising from
the inner putrefaction of an emotionally
diseased and quarrelsome nature.

❧

Questions

Three great questions arise from the beautiful, the good,
and the true: Is it lovely or ugly, true or false,
good for others and for you?

❧

Quietness

Quietness is therapeutic,
and the quest for quietness is the
cure for countless ills.

True identity is discovered in quietude;
and contentment blossoms
most profusely there.

The flower of fragrant thought
seldom blooms other than in the fields
of silence, quietness, and solitude.

Reading

Good reading bolsters every
virtue humanity craves.

A man by what he reads maps
his itinerary for tomorrow.

Reading is a form of thinking
and a stimulant to more
individual thoughts.

You will likely not be stimulated to
great thoughts by inferior reading.

Read things that are inspirational,
stimulating, and even difficult;
for soon your assimilation
will match your material.

శ

Reality

The man who learns to see deeply into the
commonplace will find reality, while others with
greater learning pass it by.

Reality has many faces, forms, and focuses but
only one essential identity of truth and function.
The reality of reality is discovered
not in examining exterior variations
or manifestations but by getting
to the heart of a thing in the most sincere
and direct manner possible.

Face life realistically, love reality,
court it like your one true love;
reform it if advisable, appraise
it accurately, accept it if possible, but never
distort it, rationalize it, or play the fool's
game of blind-man's bluff with it!

Those who reject reality and
refuse to face life lose their sense of reality
and are rejected in turn by life.

Reality is found not in the simple accumulation of facts
but by knowingly identifying with the inward essences
of manifest truth.

❧

Reason

Reason must curb passion, direct feeling, and weigh all
values, judgments, and actions in its just scales.

A woman may not always be reasonable,
but she usually has a reason for her reasoning.

Reason, although sovereign, still needs assistance
from higher levels of awareness in evaluating
sense perceptions.

He is a foolish traveler who walks a dark path
without the lamp of reason to guide his steps.

Reason was not home when self-deception and folly
auctioned life to the highest bidder for a song.

Reason should always ride herd
on the trail drive of animal instincts, emotions,
desires, and human behavior.

❧

Recompense

Happy is the man who radiates goodwill, tolerance,
kindness, and peace; for what he projects rebounds to
him again like a basketball from the backboard
of just compensation.

ॐ
Recreation

They learn to work best who learn to play well;
and recreation should properly include relaxation,
entertainment, amusement, creative activity, and play!

Fortunate is the man whose recreation and work are one.

Man is a social creature, not just a moneymaking
machine; he must straighten his aching back, breathe in
the fresh air outdoors, and learn to look anew
and enjoy the world in which he lives.

The productive brain must be productively fed on a
well-balanced, invigorating diet of variety and high quality.

True recreation is not dissipation, but a creating anew
of perfect mental, spiritual, and physical efficiency
and well-being.

Recreation stimulates aspiration; and the subconscious
mind does its best work while the conscious mind and
body are pleasantly but not too strenuously occupied.

A man soon knows if his recreation is vitalizing or
depleting his vital forces. He may best judge his
choice of recreation when it provides new
vitality, fresh insight, brighter outlook,
increased knowledge, and renewed joy for living.

162

Well-chosen recreation fortifies our fitness,
increases and prolongs our usefulness, and gears the
human mind to the tempo of action and achievement.

Recreation for the ambitious is often found
by temporary change of pace, activity,
interest, and attention, after which the
mind and body, refreshed and invigorated,
return eagerly to their primary objective.

~

Reflection

To reflect upon the efficient organization of our time
might well give us more time for further reflection.

Reflection is the art of bouncing an idea against the
backboard of past experience, accumulated knowledge,
and intuitive wisdom until we see it from every angle in
relationship to the present, the past, and the intuitively
anticipated future.

Reflection is casting the light of past experience,
memory, reason, and wonder upon the present point
of concentration.

Continued reflection often brings lucid insight into
depths of being and purpose unknown to those
who only think superficially.

Reflection on a thought gives the mind
time to evaluate it, adapt it, classify it,
and file it for future use and reference.

No one should swallow what he doesn't intend to digest.

Meditation, reflection, and creative thought should
become a mental habit — a way of observing
and evaluating life experience.

Reflection and concentration add wattage
to the lamps by which we read. They can illuminate
the meaning of a paragraph and open a door
through the printed page into the writer's thought
and unexpressed communication.

~

Relaxation

The Great Creator, who put man's machinery together in
the first place, knew it must be oiled daily with positive,
grateful attitudes and that the alarm on his timepiece
should be shut off one day in every seven.

~

Reliability

A reputation without reliability, although excellent in
other respects, has lost its essential meaning.

Do you believe in your own dependability,
strength of purpose, and power of performance?
If you do, others will soon!

If you have a responsibility, stick to it
like a postage stamp, stay with it like a
lingering lover, labor for it like you
owned the business, and someday you will!

ॐ

Religion

Religions are to truth what cloud formations
are to sunrises and sunsets; they are
only the ever-changing
reflections of the central sun as they
come and go, but truth goes on forever.

His religion is best that makes a man's
attitude inclusive and worst if it makes
him exclusive, sectarian,
or falsely "superior."

Better to have an altar at home in your heart
with the candles of love burning than
to sit regularly in a church pew criticizing
the congregation and feeling hostile
toward all men who worship there.

An adequate religion should include, among
other things, emancipation from personal guilt
and the bondage of sin, elevation and adjustment
of self and the moral nature, the purging
and redirection of affections and desires,
the annihilation of the individual's identification
with evil, and freedom from the negativism
of his inner being with its disposition
toward rebellion against divine
sovereignty. Such a religion should arise
from, or result in, an illumined mind;
a new sense of identity, purpose, direction,
love of truth, and inner awareness of
eternal life; and an increasing understanding
of the nature of God in His invisible as well
as His manifest universe. It should make
possible for the individual an assuring
comradeship with the indwelling presence
of God, followed by a healthy, continuous growth
and accentuation of all positive, desirable virtues
in a soul climate of joy, love, peace, optimism, unselfish
sharing, and cooperative service to humanity.

&

Reputation

The man who loses his reputation,
justly or unjustly, finds himself on the
"odds and ends" table for quick disposal.

166

❧

Resentment

Resentment is the emotion of animosity that reverses
personal magnetism and strikes out enthusiasm,
cooperative achievement, and amicable relationships.

Do not stoop to resent your enemies;
but inwardly wish them well, bless them,
and, when you can reasonably do
no more, forget them; for it is by
entertaining emotional awareness of their
hurtfulness that you give them power
and help to forge the chains of bondage
that you alone must wear.

❧

Resolution

Resolutions are more easily sown than grown!

Too many resolutions have been sown in the public
thoroughfare where, even if they were not trampled
down, it would be most difficult to properly
cultivate, protect, and water them,
or to gather a harvest.

Successful resolutions equal strong incentives
plus persistence.

To resolve is insufficient; action is the best proof
of intention, and performance is the test of ability.

Without resolution, the human mind is a
great "slumber mill" with opportunities
piled high like logs but with no wheels
turning, no saws cutting, and no
finished lumber in the yards.
Resolution in action can change this into a
"lumber mill" alive with purposeful activity
and personal profit!

ॐ

Responsibility

Responsibility accepted and duty attended
make achievement expected for effort expended.

Every common day should be a rehearsal for future
responsibility; and good preparation
obviates hard reparation.

ॐ

Rest

The person who rests well works best.

Repose is more to be found within the heart than to be
achieved from a change of outward circumstance.

A good conscience can sleep better on corncobs and
confidence than injustice on its feather bed
of banknotes, greenbacks, and greed!

❧

Retaliation

The retaliatory person picks at wounds
that would more quickly heal if he could
but forgive and forget their cause.

Every sales prospect who becomes a sales
victim, not a satisfied customer,
can be counted on to advertise the
product gladly without remuneration.
He may even consider himself a public
defender devoid of retaliation.

❧

Revenge

The heart that beats with malice needs
a replacement equipped with the
pacemaker called love!

Revenge is social anarchy. Human progress
and social well-being depend on the
golden rule of love, forgiveness, goodwill,
and helpfulness.

Those noble minds who do not stoop to revenge
or petty retaliation have no rattling skeletons
in their closets to disturb their serenity.

આ

Rules

When conduct is too restricted,
rebellion can accurately be predicted.
We'd sooner graduate from "hard-knocks school"
if we learned to practice the golden rule.

❧
Safety

If safety were the first rule of success,
no ship would leave the harbor, no soldier would go to
battle, and few wrongs or wants would be
fearlessly challenged; but adventure, progress,
and desire necessitate the courageous facing
of the unpredictable in man's
insistent conquest of life.

Safety has less to do with dangerous
circumstances than with the outer protection
of inner confidence and the invulnerable
armor of courage and faith.

❧
Salesmanship

The man who oversells himself simply advertises
his present insecurity and need for reassurance.

A successful salesman must motivate the
buyer and generate in him deep, persistent,
directed desires.

An indomitable
will to win is the secret of great
salesmanship.

There aren't enough "no"
responses in any earthly language
to permanently discourage the man who
sincerely wants to become a master salesman.

To sell successfully, lay a good foundation
of customer understanding; then
enthusiastically create desire, want, and
hunger for the benefits and end results
of your product.

People buy because they would rather say yes than
no, and especially if it is to their advantage to do so.

Create desire to buy through appealing to the customer's
basic want of health, wealth, admiration, security,
amusement, self-improvement, or whatever you
discern to be his motive. Relate the advantages of
what you sell to what he most instinctively
wants and needs. If potential need is lacking,
you don't have a prospect in the first place.

Let the salesman be instinctively aware of buying signals.
When these are observed, begin immediately to push
gently and persistently for a decision.

If customer response and buying signals are insufficient,
and if desire and interest are not strong enough,
backtrack, restate benefits, and resell before
attempting to close the sale.

The buyer will often courteously
help you make the close easy when he
fully understands the ways of obtaining
believable benefits, provided your
enthusiasm and believability have
fanned his wants and sense of need
to a white-heated flame.

Closing a sale is a thrill, a beautiful art,
and a natural consequence if an
effective presentation precedes it.

తి

Satisfaction

Life is a mountain to climb, not a bed
to sleep in; and those who are
too easily satisfied are too often
unaware of the possibilities.

Satisfied desires only move over to make room for more.

The triunity of man's being cries out for satisfaction
in the wisdom of truth, the revelation of the good,
and the sense-apprehended beauty of the
natural, each in its proper proportion;
and if the distilled essence of the best
cannot satisfy man's inner being, there is little
hope that the sordid sewage of the distorted senses
alone can satisfy it adequately.

ॐ

Savings

The habit of thrift results in savings plus interest
plus the virtues of self-denial, self-discipline,
self-confidence, and self-respect.

A man should certainly save any present, unexpected
income against the future's unexpected want!

If you're willing to kiss your life-saving adieu,
just let some smooth promoter get next to you!

ॐ

Scandal

If you could blow out a scandal like you can blow out
candles, it would be dark everywhere.

174

❧

Security

Security is found more in self-improvement
than in self-seeking accumulation.

Man's real security is found in his
knowledge of access
to divine supply through an
appropriating faith.

A right concept of God gives a real sense of security.

❧

Self

The closer we cling to self,
the more loosely we hold to God;
those who would possess all of God
must consecrate all of self.

❧

Self-Analysis

Your first business is to know what you are,
why you're not something else,
where you could improve, and why you should;
but how to accomplish the reformation
is the biggest challenge.

If we could constructively criticize
ourselves with the same candid accuracy
that we criticize our enemies,
we'd either make immediate improvement
or become strangely allergic to mirrors!

To know yourself is to understand all humanity;
for human similarities are greater than human differences
though not as obvious.

The man who understands himself can help himself;
and those who have helped themselves
are best qualified to help others.
Honesty is the first prerequisite of
valid self-improvement.

≈

Self-Conceit

True greatness pays court to modesty
but avoids those common broads called
conspicuousness, conceit, and self-exhibition.

≈

Self-Confidence

Action puts fear to flight and builds self-confidence.

The truest self-confidence is based on God-confidence.

Those who think on the courage of heroes endure
until the end of the day.

Self-confidence, not self-sufficiency, holds hands
with Divinity and walks fearlessly
through the darkness to the light.

Self-confidence, although courageous,
must be tempered with self-control and sincere humility.

Only the confident inspire confidence;
and only the success-conscious become conscious
of success in fact and in reality.

Self-confidence is a fine balance between fact and
faith, between what we have done and what we
know we can do, and between what we actually
are and what we are potentially.

Self-confidence, if rooted in reality,
is a tree that the storm may bend but never break.

Don't limp because you almost broke your leg;
be glad you didn't, and walk taller than ever before.

Run a check on the frequency of
"but, if, and maybe" in your
conversation and it will give you
a fairly accurate self-confidence rating.

Better to start mixing mortar and
carrying God than to start at the top
and play like you *are* God.
Self-confidence, like most virtues,
has built-in limitations.

༜

Self-Control

Let every man become a king; let every vagrant desire
answer at Reason's Gate before he enters the kingdom;
and let all emotion be in loyal subjection
without commotion.

༜

Self-Denial

A little self-denial in the morning of life
may save a lot of deprivation at the end of the day.

༜

Self-Determination

I am a free man! I can do whatever I want
with the consent of my conscience, the Church,
the Federal Government, State law, public consensus
of opinion, civil rights, custom, precedence,
circumstances, finances, time, health,
ability, and my wife!

❧
Self-Direction

Why drive fast if you don't know where you are going?

❧
Self-Doubt

Self-doubt is traitor to our best interests.
It discounts our hopes and dreams and sells our
birthright of success in the marketplace of despair
for an IOU of consolation.

❧
Self-Education

Self-education often finds its greatest inspiration and
profit from biography and the history of achievement.

The man without any funds for tuition
can still find a free library at his disposition.

The self-discipline required is part of the self-education
desired by all who would continue to learn.

The person who is not interested in
continuing his self-education after graduation,
and who hides behind his "sheepskin," is
likely to be dispatched by the wolves of competition
who hunger for his position and his pay.

֍

Self-Examination

An honest self-examination could
readily produce a reformation and,
better yet, a transformation, if we would
face the inner reality of our introspection
with a view to its correction.

֍

Self-Image

The sinner who forgives himself
finds it much easier to forgive his neighbor.

A man's conduct is quite consistent with
the image and opinion he holds of
himself sincerely and subjectively.

The person who condemns and criticizes himself
unduly is contributing to his own delinquency
and the suicide of his better self.

In the drama of life, people choose the
part they play, direct the production,
and win the applause of their
conscience and the audience only when
they are genuinely pleased with the
true quality of their performance.

Pictorially review the day's doings
before sleep and picture it not as it was
but vividly revised
as you now wish it might have been;
for from these new visual chartings
tomorrow's deeds will be automatically directed.
Purposeful review and revisions
affect tomorrow's self-image and decisions.

ॐ

Self-Improvement

The propelling, impelling motive of all
nature is the desire for advancement,
improvement, and increase of life!

Directed attention and simple
awareness are the intuitive, appropriative
processes of attaining wisdom, position,
information, wealth, power, health,
acceptance, and general self-improvement.
For example: to direct the attention to,
and become aware of confidence is to
discern its qualities and to identify
with its positive feelings. To emotionally
identify with something is to
possess its qualities first subjectively in
essence and then objectively in
manifest reality.

ॐ
Selfishness

Selfishness stands outside the Garden of Eden
with a half-eaten apple in its hand watching
the worm of disillusionment crawl
serpent-like out of its hollow core!

ॐ
Self-Reliance

The meaning of self-reliance is found more on
the battlefield of experience than in the pages
of the lexicon.

Self-reliance springs from the seed of the will to win
that has been planted by faith, watered by hope,
and cultivated courageously until the harvest comes.

Self-doubt is a parasite, but self-reliance is a sturdy tree;
and men make lumber from forests, not fungus!

The man without self-reliance who adjusts
too readily to every public demand
will soon need his own chiropractor
to identify and readjust his dislocated parts.

Always be a learner but not a leaner; and remember that
the crowd moves over for the man who moves in.

William R. Jackson

Self-reliance, if it courageously concentrates
its drive, is usually crowned with cooperation
or just crowned!

Self-reliance is compatible with God-entrusted
self-sovereignty, free moral agency,
self-direction, self-confidence, and
the intuitive wisdom that
knows where to go for help.

Man must depend upon his inner self, knowing that his
inner self may securely depend upon higher powers.

The first rule for self-reliance is
the awareness of invisible and visible
allies and our ability to direct
and command all available forces within
and without to win decisive victories.

No man should be weak or fearful
when he fully realizes that God and the
Kingdom of Heaven are both within him.

God himself knows that we may need
a helping hand; that's why he gave us
two of our own. He no doubt also believes
that all men should have equal opportunities
on which to stand, and that's why
he gave us two feet!

❧
Self-Respect

Self-respect battles against uneven odds
when it battles unsuccessfully against unpaid debts
and unacknowledged obligations.

❧
Sensitiveness

Even the blind mole is sensitive enough to know
when someone walks over him, trespasses on his private
diggings, or when some shadow obscures the warmth
of unseen light as he surfaces for a moment in the sun.

❧
Service

Any station in life should be a service station,
whether the attendant wears coveralls, cap and gown,
or the robes of royalty.

Those who serve the best deserve the most!

All those who serve should receive from the reserve
a just share of profit to spend or preserve.

To share is a sacrament; to serve is fulfillment;
and to love humanity is to be in fellowship with God.

184

❧

Silence

In solitude's rarefied atmosphere a man
can feel his greatest humility, assess his
truest talents with the surest degree
of candor, and perceive his foremost
duty with the utmost clarity.

Solitude speaks a silent language known
only to nature, the listening soul,
and the Great Creator.

Silence is essential to nobility of mind and heart.

Out of the soil of silence the greatest virtues grow,
and the secrets of life are seldom revealed
to the crowd rushing to and fro.

❧

Simplicity

How many unnecessary things could you delete
in order to do better the things that count?

Simplify!

Affectation reaches for greatness
but simplicity possesses it.

Those who understand the best
can explain even the difficult with amazing simplicity;
but those who only think they know
can make simplicity itself seem incomprehensible.

❧

Sin

It is natural to sin, commendable to forsake it,
but wise to avoid it!

❧

Sleep

Insomnia often flees when the sleeper is on his knees!

❧

Smile

A genuine smile creates goodwill and inspires
inner optimism and self-confidence in the person
smiling, and it usually makes the day brighter
for the observer, especially if he
is capable of responding.

If only half of the exhortations to smile had been
put into practice, you would probably have a lot
of people smiling on only one side of their face;
but even that would help some if you knew how to
get on the good side of them.

❧

Smoking

Smoking is a wonderful cure for some things—
ham in particular.

Smoking must be great because so many
people are willing to pay for the privilege
and throw their lungs
into the bargain to boot!

❧

Society

All society tends to classify itself into uppers and lowers;
but if the lowers were uppers and the uppers were lowers
it still wouldn't solve the problem, for both seem
necessary if man wants to eat. This is equally true
if you're talking about false teeth.

Society will always reflect the average quality
and collective identity of the individuals who compose it.
When we condemn it, we pronounce sentence
upon ourselves at least to some degree.

❧

Sorrow

Sorrow is an ocean that beats on every shore.

Grief is an empty house
haunted by memories of what it no longer holds.

❧

Speaking

Speak kindly with your eyes, clearly with your lips,
and sincerely from your heart and you shall be
both heard and remembered.

Words weighed in judgment and voiced in kindness are
sturdy seeds planted in the garden of the hearers that will
produce fragrance and fruitage in due season.

The mental impulse of thought reaches the midbrain
of another before the sound can reach the ear
or the meaning of words be translated
by the conscious mind. If such thought and words
do not agree, confusion arises; but the thought
transferred takes priority in the listener's emotional
response. Therefore, let all men think sincerely
and speak accordingly
to be most clearly understood.

Let the tone of your voice speak goodwill
and the thought spoken will be more readily received;
for man's self-protective instinct reacts to moods
more quickly than to meanings.

188

༈

Speculation

Those who greedily grab for a get-rich-quick
scheme usually find they have a
wildcat by the tail and come out generally
holding the short end of it!

How long since you have walked
through the Cemetery of Speculation
and read the epitaphs on the tombstones
of your past financial folly?

༈

Strategy

Don't cry for courage when strategy serves best.

༈

Strength

Courage is the medicine
that brings health to the disease called weakness.

The individual that too readily confesses to being a
worm will likely feel the impulse to crawl again.
The strong choose different symbols for their
totem poles of courage and strength.

Those who identify with their weakness
when they could have chosen strength
have voted for defeat, difficulties,
and death. It is better to become
more conscious of our strength
than of our weakness, of our
possibilities than our problems.

❧

Success

Success City is a place of positive attitudes,
subjective assurance, projected vision,
persistent desire, creative thought,
and enduring labor.

Success is a manner and a mood of traveling
as much as a destination.

The man who thinks success is
only material gain will find a false bottom
in his basket on Judgment Day.

❧

Suggestion

The self-directed person learns to control his own
suggestibility so that he responds primarily to what
he feels is good for him, and rejects automatically and

instinctively what may affect him adversely.
Because he values his free moral agency, the wise
individual is alert to guard against obvious or subliminal
suggestive influences around him that would
unconsciously influence him to accept what he
would not consciously choose.

The unwary absorb the painful or pleasant
emotional coloring that others attach to the
factual material presented for their
consideration. This, if unchallenged, prejudices
judgment and predetermines decisions
relative to the factual material which, without another
person's biased emotional coloring, might well have
been accepted or rejected on its own merit.

The sentinels of reason and judgment
must never sleep at their post of duty
where they protect and screen influences
of thought and emotions that would otherwise
contaminate the instinctive inner mind which
automatically executes the inherent activity
of an idea accepted by it.

Every form of communication carries both
direct and subtle suggestion intended to curb or
direct our powers of self-determination. It is a
fortunate person who can detect and resist
unwanted influences at the threshold.

Our facts can be gathered from many sources,
but our emotions and reactions should arise
unprejudiced from within.

It is often best to neither deny nor admit an undesired
condition, but simply to ignore the negative and affirm
wholeheartedly the positive desirable condition.

Any suggestion given by others or self-administered
is more effective in rhythmic form and with happy,
subjective emotional quality, but without strain
or excessive effort.

Self-suggestion purposefully sown in the subconscious
mind is often defeated because we "talk out" to others
what should be left to incubate in silence
and be fulfilled in its proper time and place.

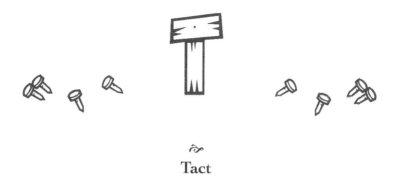

Tact

Tact is an acute sense of social awareness,
propriety, wise judgment, and well-timed improvisation.

Tact without talent may accomplish more
than talent devoid of tact.

The tactful comply graciously with necessity and
cooperate courteously with the inevitable when they are
unable to blow up the opposition with finesse.

Talents

Every man is given some gift
to exchange in the marketplace.

Hidden talents rust without reward.

Talents or ability, like money, have little value
unless put into circulation.

༃

Talking

Temperance should begin with the telephone.

If talking were intoxicating,
half the women in the world would be dead drunk.

Pure water never intoxicated any man
or loosened his tongue unwisely.

All speech courses should begin with the art of listening
and end with the virtue of brevity.

The brevity of your speaking may reveal the extent
of your comprehension.

Depth of understanding does not always determine
the length of the explanation; but time, good judgment,
and circumstances should.

Speakers who are too much given to details are not too
often given the opportunity to voice their
tedious digressions.

Talk may be cheap, but its consequences are costly
to the careless who cannot curb it.

It is easier to talk without thinking
than to think without talking.

No matter how versatile the tongue,
it is better to lose its use than to use it loosely.

They seldom work diligently who talk incessantly.

No man speaks with more assumption
than the one who is really uncertain
about the few things he thinks he knows.

Who feels like gossiping in solitude
where even the trees whisper wordlessly to the
vagrant breezes passing by? Thus nature teaches
the virtue of silence to those who are close to God.

୭

Taste

Good taste, like tact, arises from an intuitive sense
of propriety; and circumstances may sharpen or dull it,
but early habits resist reform.

୭

Teaching

Only the taught should be teachers,
for empty baskets carry no bread.

It is better to teach students than
simply to teach facts.

To be taught how to learn is more important than
being taught what others think we ought to know.

Those who teach best do not pour water into empty
cisterns but open artesian wells within!

The school is a blacksmith shop;
and only when interest and love of learning are
white-heated at the forge of enthusiasm
can the educator temper the steel of desire
and shape the purpose of useful living.

What a pity that the maladjusted, the incompetent,
or the biologically unfit should ever become teachers
of tomorrow's citizenry!

༂

Teamwork

Teamwork is the ability to subordinate personal drive
to group interest and achievement;
and the man whose attitude says,
"I want to work with and for others,"
is a teamworker.

The teamworker is less egocentric,
more cooperation conscious, more inclined to service
than to selfishness; and although he is sacrificing
some independence, he is every inch a man.

William R. Jackson

Tears

Tears wash the eyes of error
and teach the soul to see.

The silent tear speaks volumes
to those who care to read.

Better to share the treasure of your tears
in compassion here and there
than to save a miser's hoard
to spend on your own despair.

It is wiser to release emotion in
silent tears than to blow off the
steam of repressed anger.

No words conceive such eloquence
as when the eyes give birth to tears.

Courage shines like a priceless jewel
when the rainbow of hope is reflected
in the refraction of a tear.

Let the good man who dries a widow's tears
bring a life preserver
lest he be too soon carried away
on the tide.

ॐ
Telepathy

All people hear more than sound, see more than sight,
and feel instinctively the emotions and thoughts
that others subconsciously project.

ॐ
Temperance

He who worships the dinner table and values little
the art of temperance and good health
has doubtful cause to thank God for his intended
and habitual gluttony.

ॐ
Temptation

Temptation is like quicksand; those who hesitate
a moment on its margin are caught before they are fully
aware of the danger, and sink silently
even as they struggle to survive.

ॐ
Thankfulness

"Thank you" is a magic word,
but say it twice so you're sure it's heard!

꙰

Theology

The best theology is sacrifice and service;
the poorest is self-centered complacency.

꙰

Thinking

The halo of the thinker is soon seen
above the milling crowd; and so are the tomatoes
and cabbages they throw to humiliate the proud.

Your eyes are the picture tubes
for the television of the soul.

Independence thinks for itself; love thinks of others;
but tyranny tries to do the other man's thinking for him.

To think in images recalled is not difficult, for it is often
little more than reminiscence. To think in abstractions is
more difficult still, for principles and ideas are harder to
hold even when translated into symbols. But to think
intuitively is the easiest, yet the most difficult of all,
for its processes are the most illusive and its wisdom
is the soonest escaped unless captured
as the inspiration takes wings at the
hidden womb of creative thought.

ॐ
Thought

Thought is an artist whose idle doodlings
become tomorrow's blueprints; and thought is a dreamer
whose fantasy becomes tomorrow's history.

Thought enamored with virile action
leads to the trysting place of creativity.

There is no birth of progress
without the parenthood of thought.

To understand cause is better than to beg for effects.

Thought like the thunderbolt
should set dead trees aflame.

Positive and virile thoughts
have great displacement value
and are even welcomed by vacuity itself.

ॐ
Time

Time is the soul of eternity, but too often it is lost.

The clock of time runs slow, or so it often seems;
but life is sooner over than the careless mortal dreams.

The greatest penalty for time wasted is the death of
ambition as we judge ourselves unworthy of reward.

Man works eight hours, sleeps eight hours,
and has eight hours left; but it is what he thinks of
during the first sixteen and what he does with
the last eight that make the real difference.

Time is more valuable with advancing age,
not only because there is less of it
but because of the accumulated interest
of increased potential.

It is amazing that men should even hope for success
when they gave so little time to promote it.

❧

Timidity

Timidity is a termite that undermines audacity,
crumbles our confidence, and reduces opportunity
to the sawdust of futility.

❧

Today

Today is an expectant mother;
tomorrow is an unborn child. It could be a genius
or a dullard; it's how you feed the fetus today that counts.

Today is one day; tomorrow is another;
yet the future is the offspring and
today will be its mother.

Today is a good day; it's a new day;
for some things it's creation's day
and for other things it's doomsday;
but for all things it's our day,
and it can be our best day.

❧

Tolerance

The man who can't tolerate himself
is most intolerant of others.

Since tolerance is a difficult virtue,
let's make it easy for the other person to tolerate us.

❧

Tomorrow

Tomorrow is the boot-hill cemetery
for alibis and the unmarked grave
of stillborn ambitions.

There never has been a tomorrow, for it comes
rechristened "Today," so now is the time for action.
It's the future that is slipping away.

At midnight the rose of tomorrow blooms
with its fragrance bold; and sunrise will greet it
with dewdrops of hope,
brighter than diamonds or gold.

❧

Trade

The man who borrows a dozen eggs to trade for a hen
is wiser than the man who trades a laying hen
for a dozen eggs.

❧

Tragedy

A lifetime of integrity is divisible by one injudicious act.
It may never add up the same again.

❧

Travel

Those who learn to observe intently wherever they are
need not travel so far or so fast
to find something worthy of observation.

❧

Tribute

Men gladly pay taxes who would never pay tribute.

203

&

Trifles

Those who make a practice of
picking at fleas usually end up
making monkeys of themselves.

Only the big boys play
in the big leagues; so who wants to be
petty or small? If you are going to play
baseball, don't practice pitching
ping-pong balls during spring training.
It pays to think big.

&

Trouble

If you claim the trouble,
you should probably claim the cause.

If your purpose and courage
are big enough, your troubles will
seem small in comparison.

Baptize your difficulties in the waters of faith,
hope, and love, and rechristen them opportunities
and such they shall be to you.

No trouble yet has turned off the sun,
blown out the stars, or frozen
the ocean of God's concern.

❧

Troublemakers

Troublemakers are "Typhoid Marys"
who should be kept in quarantine lest
their diseased emotions cause an epidemic
of distrust, despair, and disorganization.

❧

Trust

Trust that faith and truth will triumph,
for in the end they will.

The wise trust not in persons,
institutions, doctrines,
or creeds of man, but in their love
for God and man
and in God's love for man.

❧

Truth

Truth is a pilgrim, a path, and a destination.
It involves facts, the faith to find them,
and a sincere seeker dedicated to the quest.

Truth is a cement that makes the facts stick together
but has no affinity for the fabric of falsehood.

Truth is a flower whose fragrance endures forever,
while error blooms only to fade and die.
Sometimes the weeds of error must be
uprooted first so that the flowers of truth
may have freedom to fully bloom.

Truth is a staff of strength upon which the weakest may
lean with confidence, and which the strong may use
as staff, sword, and shield.

The arrow of truth will triumph, but it often lacks a
strong bow arm to direct its shaft.

No rock should stand more firmly
than our loyalty to the truth.

The courtship of truth should result in a love for reality
and the union of faith with fact.

Sincerity and unselfishness
make truth welcome anywhere.

How much the truth hurts depends upon your size,
the quality of your spirit,
and the degree of your own truthfulness.

The privilege of truth is its conformity to reality
and right where practice, not theory,
is proof of sincere acceptance.

Let truth be accepted as the
standard of thought and action.
Let it be pure, let it be strong,
let it be wise, let it be just,
let it be guileless. But above all else,
let it be sincere and complete.

More truth lies buried by the fearful
than do errors they have slain.

The man who is untrue to others
plays in truth the traitor to himself.

Revelation is a light, reason is a lamp,
and truth is the treasure found.
But reason, without divine illumination,
discovers the fool's gold of error
and dies in its cave of darkness,
unwilling to leave the false treasures
it discovered. Those who listen to the
voice of nature and observe her moods
and ways will more readily discern the
voice of truth amidst the raucous cries
of error and discord in the common marketplace.

Too many people who enjoy the search for truth
refuse to embrace it or even face it when they find it.
And, turning aside, they gather bouquets of error
to place on the grave of their lost sincerity.

ॐ
Truthfulness

Truthfulness conceived and born in the light
has no part with deception
which was spawned in the darkness.

Of what virtue is the knowledge of truth
without the practice of truthfulness; or what is its value
in the abstract if it is not manifest in the practical.

How women arrive so unerringly at truth
with such insufficient evidence and by such unorthodox
reasoning is truly amazing and not without cause for
both consolation and consternation; but let it be
remembered that the intuitive mind and truthfulness
are very much akin.

❧

Ugliness

Even ugliness has beauty
in the eyes of love.

❧

Unbelief

Faith is a Jacob's ladder that leads
from earth to heaven; but unbelief would
cut it down, round by round.

The hammer and anvil of cold argument
can seldom dent the exterior of unbelief.
Only the fires of faith, love, and desire
can melt it into a golden river
of confidence and compliance.

Unbelief is rooted in the dark soil of rebellion,
and there is no cure for it except the God-stimulated
exercise of man's sovereign "will to believe."

Understanding

Clarity, brevity, reflection, and interest
are sure aids to better understanding.

Union

When hearts behind united hands are one in truth,
the union stands.

To attain in this life a humble state of loving, spiritual
union with the Infinite, without the absurd error and folly
of mistaken identity, is a relationship to be
sincerely desired.

Usefulness

The decision to be useful to people
rather than to abuse people or to use people
is the test of legitimate ambition
and the secret of sincere service.

~

Valor

The courage of valor in
wisdom directed battles no
windmills in the targets selected.

Courage is not an old blind horse
driven tremblingly up to the precipice
brink in uncertainty and fear.
True valor is Pegasus with spread
wings glinting in the morning
sun, with arched neck, flowing mane,
and rippling muscles of steel, whose
pawing feet strike sparks from the
gravel on the chasm's edge
as he crouches for the confident
leap with eyes on the other side
unmindful of the winding river
and the treetops far below.

Values

All men must live awhile, and all must die;
but what we choose to live and die for
indicates the validity of our values.

All values will arrange themselves
more harmoniously around the center of our
being when we have found
our place in the center of Divine Being.

Vanity

When distorted vanity too hungry grows,
its octopus nature its greediness shows.

Variety

The conformity of variety and the variety
of conformity give unity to diversity and
a pattern to inconsistency.

Victory

Victory holds the seeds of false content, for complacency
spawns its vices after victory's gains are spent.

212

❧

Virtue

Women of virtue are always chaste;
and those without it are too often chased!

Virtue blighted by false vanity is a dying vine.
Let virtue in another win applause
as much as when you say, "It's mine!"

There is a great value even in virtue maintained by
unwanted circumstance; but the truest virtue
is the fruit of constant and purified desires.

❧

Virus

A wise man with an irritating tack in his shoe's sole
removes it; but the unwise man with an irritating emotion
in his inner soul harbors, nurses, and keeps it as his own
until its non-spiritual virus destroys
both his body and his soul!

❧

Vision

Never let faith's vision die, lest hope expire as well.
For with faith and hope and vision dead,
there's little left to tell.

❧
Want

A man may adjust his wants by tightening his belt
or indulge them by loosening his purse.

Man's wants, whether based on need or simply desire,
will find expression in some form or die trying.

❧
Waste

The man who wastes the wages of his work
wastes with it a measure of his self-confidence,
peace of mind, self-respect, and security.

The habit of thrift and the quality of character
arising from self-denial are of more value than the
balance in a savings account,
however small or large.

Those who save, save more than money!

Some hounds, who might lead the pack
in the fox hunt for success, are kept back
by the collar and chain of want arising
from unwise waste of time and money.

To waste the unwanted is sometimes wiser
than to want the unwasted for the sake of
unwise frugality. Remember the packrat.

☙

Watch

It might be well to rewind our purpose
when we wind the unwound watch!

☙

Weakness

Examining the symptoms of a disease may be necessary
for a diagnosis; but continued contemplation of weakness
and want is the cause of failure, not its cure.

☙

Wealth

In our youth we want wealth, health, and happiness.
In middle age we want happiness, wealth, and health.
The order in old age is health, happiness,
and enough to live comfortably.

Weight

Dieting is simply a matter of mind over platter!

Will

Willpower is desire plus reason plus resolution.

Willpower is self-directed vital force
awakened by necessity, chance, or aspiration.

The life of the will is the will to live.

The will is the ability to decide, to persist in a wisely
calculated decision, and the source of
self-controlled conduct.

The spirit of cooperation is the catalyst in the will that is
diplomatically tactful. Desire is the heart of the will that is
magnetically attractive. Command is the key to the will
that consciously controls others, while comprehensive,
expansive awareness of creative energy held in
abeyance is the will that dominates collectively.
This control force is felt in the non-muscular tension
and feeling of readiness preceding action or emergency
and is the thought-feeling that encompasses individuals,
crowds, circumstances, cities, and even nations.

The will may be exercised with increased
efficiency in the prompt doing of necessary
but disagreeable things, or by refusing the
easy thing that is not in our
ultimate best interest.

Any unnecessary self-delay in purposeful action
weakens the will when once the course has
wisely been decided upon.

The will may be strengthened by awareness
arising from contemplation of its nature and manner,
or reward of action.

Silent, inner willing is often the
wisest way of winning.

To want, to will, to work,
and to wait is to finally win.

Willfulness may be nothing more than
obstinacy unable emotionally to choose
freely the course of action best suited
to its own self-interests.

❧

Wings

Those who pray for wings should also ask for directions.

꙳
Wisdom

Wisdom is the reflected light of truth that reveals
the oneness of the past cause, the present content, and the
future consequences of the considered course of action.

All the college degrees in the world can't give you true
wisdom; it is the quintessence of experience, the
distillation of adversity; and without adversity, wisdom is
wanting. Those who learn suffer some things and
those who suffer with discernment learn wisdom.

It is better to learn wisdom by intuition
than to confirm it by the unnecessary suffering
of unwise experience.

Painful knowledge, not wisdom,
is the doubtful fruit of folly.

The silent owl who seldom speaks is the symbol of
wisdom, not the parrot who parades his meaningless
reiterations to every passerby.

꙳
Wit

The wit that wilts and withers what it wants to win
is the verbal folly in the courtship of fools.

William R. Jackson

≈

Woman

With Adam's rib
God mixed in earth the fragrance of flowers,
the bitterness of herbs, the sweetness of wild honey,
the stardust of dreams and fire,
fashioned it in perfection, breathed on it with love,
and waking Adam softly said,
"This is woman!"

≈

Work

Let today's work compete with yesterday's tally,
and let each effort be the greatest conquest
when it's done.

With six days of work neglected,
even the Creator couldn't rest on the seventh.

Even those who succeed through genius
like to make believe it was all hard work;
but inspired work done willingly
is the truest pleasure
in spite of any difficulty.

The blessed curse of labor has saved the race
from the ruin of protracted idleness and utter discontent.

More than half our hours are spent in labor, for labor and
life are one; and those who refuse to work productively
have ceased to live fully.

There is no work as unrewarding
as the effort to avoid the boredom of idleness
while enduring the weariness of want.

Work is less than labor and more than doing
when the joy of achievement and the will to work is in it.

Work is the backlog in the fireplace of genius,
the underground river that feeds the springs of
prosperity, the steel girders under the hardwood
floors, and the plush carpets of success.

Work is a privilege at whatever pay; for our help is not
needed half so much as we need a place to worship God
and grow by serving and loving our fellow man.

He who is wholeheartedly devoted to duty
is dutifully devoted to God.

Action and ambition awaken the giant of inspiration
and stir the blood of conquest in the veins of the man
who is willing to work.

God keeps us aware of the urgency of life,
the brevity of time, and the necessity
of working early and late.

William R. Jackson

Arise and attack the task; for no work will ever be done
unless something or someone does it.

Judge not a man altogether by the nature of his task
as much as by the manner of its performance.

Work, by the nature of its exercise, produces an amazing
capacity for more work with greater ease.

There are too many fields with the corners still unplowed;
keep your furrows straight and your fence corners clean.

Help somebody going somewhere and you become
somebody doing something.
Usefulness is a virtue of infinite worth.

To work willingly and to wait patiently
is to achieve lastingly.

Good work results in greater ability to do still better
work, and the increase in quality is better
than increased quantity.

Ambition must run its own interference
while ability and consistent effort
trip the electric eye that opens every door.

Inventory the assets of your abilities
and invest the dividends of your achievement
and you will reap the rewards of your labors.

The shining plowshare rusts away
not from turning furrows but from disuse.

What man can fashion, time can tarnish;
for nothing man-made is eternal.

෨

Worry

Worry is blind negativism, exaggerated fear,
and the diseased function of an inactive will
too weary to get off the nightmare treadmill
of self-doubt and inner despair.

Worry is a monster behind the mask
of every man's face who hasn't
conquered devitalizing self-depreciation
with its hidden face of fear.

Worry is emotional cannibalism,
and the bone you gnaw on is your own.

Worry is growing anxiety,
the lurking fear of uncertainty,
and insecurity caught in the dilemma
of indecision.

Worry is mental indigestion caused from the vitamin
deficiency of courage, faith, hope, and quiet confidence.

The worry-furrowed brow advertises, "I don't know
where I'm going or why, and if I did, I doubt if I'd
really make it, and especially not on time!"

The man who worries pays a high rate of interest in
advance on troubles expected but which may never come.

The man with self-confident courage is a tempered,
steel instrument with a razor-sharp edge
well suited for any close shave.

Fear flees at the footsteps of faith, and hopelessness
cannot endure the happy songs of gratitude.

Worry doubts the outcome before the race begins.

Nothing cures worry and grim despair like exercise,
sleep, sunshine, and fresh air.

Nature is never worried, and all wildlife
seems to work in patient rhythm at the
task of survival, unplagued by
all the frantic fears that wiser
mortals know.

☙

Writing

A man must live a book before he can write one!

A writer is an artist who puts
new pictures in old frames, old pictures
in new frames, new pictures in new frames,
and leaves some pictures without frames
and some frames without pictures
in hopes he can inspire the creative thought
and action of the readers and stimulate their
desire to evaluate the finished work,
the complete and incomplete, and to
comprehend in an hour what it took a
lifetime to learn and portray.

ఇ

X-Rays

The illumined mind, like an X-ray, penetrates exteriors,
discovers inner structures, and throws its light upon the
interiors, the essences, and realities
of this broken thing called life.

❧

Yearnings

If our yearning capacity didn't exceed our
earning capacity, our ulcers wouldn't
have such churning capacity.

❧

Yesterday

Our yesterdays are never lost;
they labor by our side today
and add to our rewards tomorrow.

Yesterday is a morgue of dead dreams; forget them.
Yesterday is a garden of flowers; smell them.
Yesterday is the seed bed of promise for all your
tomorrows; cultivate and weed them. Yesterday is the
future in disguise; work on it today and you will be proud
of it tomorrow.

Why read the epitaphs on yesterday's tombstones, or dig up the bones of past failure? Leave yesterday's shadows behind, and work in the sunlight of today's hopes and tomorrow's sure expectations.

❦

You

You is a word that shouts its individuality,
its responsibility, its opportunity, and its choice.

Only you can fully enjoy your own life,
direct your own thoughts, and determine
your ultimate success and destiny.

You have more to do with yourself than time,
circumstances, or even natural consequences.

࿓

Zealousness

The zealous are those wonderful people, if rightly
directed, who have not forgotten the meaning of ardor,
enthusiasm, earnestness, and the will to live
eagerly and with purpose.

࿓

Zephyr

The art of gentle persuasion, like the soft breeze,
enchants us with the scent of summer
without blowing up a duststorm of bitter words!